PRAISE FOR
THE BOOK OF PENDULUM HEALING

"We highly recommend *The Book of Pendulum Healing*. Joan Staffen provides a user-friendly, step-by-step guide to help anyone tap into their intuitive abilities by using the ancient and honored method of vibrational resonance. Equally important is Joan's cogent, powerfully perceptive approach to healing itself. Few of us appreciate or fully consider the multidimensional levels of causation underlying health problems and life impediments. The reader is gifted with invaluable maps and tools for fully assessing the origins of any healing issue, as well as a rich array of viable options for its resolution.

This is *not* a book you will read and then store away on some shelf to gather dust. Rather, *The Book of Pendulum Healing* will become your new best friend. It is a lifetime user's manual for how to access a deeper Core of Self; how to actualize human potential by gaining ever greater insight and mastery regarding life's challenges and inherent blessings."

—PATRICIA KAMINSKI, executive director,
Flower Essence Society, *www.flowersociety.org*

"Joan Staffen's *The Book of Pendulum Healing* is a great introduction to receiving healing guidance through the use of divination and pendulum dowsing. The tips and techniques Joan outlines will enhance one's intuition and channeling abilities."

—AMY ZERNER AND MONTE FARBER,
authors of *The Truth Fairy Pendulum Kit*
and *The Psychic Circle*

"*The Book of Pendulum Healing* is a wonderfully informative book that helps the reader delve deep into the core of their spiritual consciousness to find the answers to many of life's questions. Having been fascinated with angels for many years, I love the angelic influence in this book and all matters relating to the power of the pendulum. A must-have book for all those who have an interest in spiritual dowsing."

—LEANNA GREENAWAY, author of *Tarot Plain and Simple, Wicca Plain and Simple,* and *Wiccapedia*

"Joan Staffen takes you on an empowering journey of self-analysis and gifts you with a skill that lasts a lifetime—grab this opportunity! *The Book of Pendulum Healing* is beautifully written: Staffen's love for the divinity in all things simply zings off the page."

—ELIZABETH BROWN, author of *Dowsing: The Ultimate Guide for the 21st Century*

"Joan Rose Staffen's *The Book of Pendulum Healing* is packed with helpful tips and practical applications for pendulums in your everyday life. This book offers readers an exploration of the history and applications of dowsing by pendulum, but the more than two dozen pendulum charts are the real treasure. This is a book that you'll use time and time again in your healing practice!"

—NICHOLAS PEARSON, author of *Crystals for Karmic Healing* and *Foundations of Reiki Ryoho*

"*The Book of Pendulum Healing* by Joan Rose Staffen is chock full of insightful and practical information. This book is an excellent introduction to dowsing and provides helpful charts that the reader can use. Yet *Pendulum Healing* offers far more than simply dowsing advice. Joan's wonderful book also covers, among other topics, how to let go of limiting thoughts, how past lives can help you today, and how to deal with grief because of the death of a loved one.

The book weaves historical and factual information with Joan's own story of how she came to be a dowser and master healer. I refer to Joan as a master healer because I have benefitted from Joan's wisdom and great healing abilities. I have worked in the healing/spiritual field for two decades and met many wonderful people, but few as talented as Joan. I strongly encourage you to read this book—it will make your life better."

—CATRIONA MACGREGOR, award-winning
author of *Partnering with Nature: The Wild Path
to ReConnecting with the Earth*, spiritual guide, and
founder of Nature Quest®

THE BOOK OF
PENDULUM
HEALING

THE BOOK OF
PENDULUM HEALING

*Charting Your
Healing Course for
Mind, Body, and Spirit*

JOAN ROSE STAFFEN

WEISER BOOKS

This edition first published in 2019 by Weiser Books, an imprint of
Red Wheel/Weiser, LLC

With offices at:
65 Parker Street, Suite 7
Newburyport, MA 01950
www.redwheelweiser.com

All quotes from *A Course in Miracles* are from the 1986 edition, first published in 1975 by
the Foundation for Inner Peace, P.O. Box 598, Mill Valley, CA 94942-598, *www.acim.org* and
info@acim.org.

Disclaimer: This book contains advice and information relating to pendulums, crystals,
foods, vitamins, minerals, and flower essences and is not meant to diagnose, treat, or prescribe. It should be used to supplement, not replace, the advice of your physician or other
trained healthcare practitioner. If you know or suspect you have a medical condition, are
experiencing physical symptoms, or if you feel unwell, seek your physician's advice before
embarking on any medical program or treatment. Readers using the information in this book
do so entirely at their own risk, and the author and publisher accept no liability if adverse
effects are caused.

ISBN: 978-1-57863-636-5

Library of Congress Cataloging-in-Publication Data available upon request.

Cover design by Kathryn Sky-Peck
Cover photograph by Matthias Kulka/Corbis Collection/Getty Images
Interior images by Joan Rose Staffen
Interior by Maureen Forys, Happenstance Type-O-Rama
Typeset in Trajan, Cronos, and Adobe Jenson

Printed in Canada

MAR

10 9 8 7 6 5 4 3 2 1

*To my wonderful clients
who courageously share their
healing journeys with me*

All healing is a release from fear.

—*A COURSE IN MIRACLES*

Throughout history, men and women characterized
as diviners, dowsers, soothsayers, seers, mystics,
mediums, clairvoyants, shamans, witch doctors,
wizards & etc., have developed and practiced arts
regarded as divine or demonic (depending on the
viewpoint) and are able to answer questions that
logical reason could not provide. In essence, these
people through self training, diligent practice and a
profound knowledge of how the universe really func-
tioned, simply "knew things" via the faculty of what
has been called the "hidden senses" or E.S.P.

—CHRISTOPHER BIRD, *The Divining Hand*

I know very well that many scientists consider
dowsing as they do astrology, as a type of ancient
superstition. According to my conviction this is,
however, unjustified. The dowsing rod is a simple
instrument which shows the reaction of the human
nervous system to certain factors which are
unknown to us at this time.

—ALBERT EINSTEIN,
Letter to Mr. Herman E. Peisach, 1946

CONTENTS

LIST OF INTUITIVE
HEALING CHARTS

FOUNDATION CHARTS

Yes/No and Clearing Signal
(Chart 1)

Time and Percent (Chart 2)

Seek and Find Spirit (Chart 3)

Spiritual Guides (Chart 4)

Energy Body—Auric Layers
(Chart 5)

Chakras (Chart 6)

Physical Body (Chart 7)

Body Systems (Chart 8)

Type of Healing Needed (Chart 9)

HEALTH CHALLENGES

Factors Contributing to Disease
(Chart 10)

Life Stressors (Chart 11)

Addictions (Chart 12)

Blocks to Healing (Chart 13)

Limiting Thoughts (Chart 14)

HEALING SOLUTIONS

Empowering Thoughts (Chart 15)

Clearing Needed (16)

Feelings (Chart 17)

Human Needs (Chart 18)

Self-Care (Chart 19)

Healing Arts (Chart 20)

Food (Chart 21)

Vitamins and Minerals (Chart 22)

Flower Essences (Chart 23)

Aromatherapy (Chart 24)

Crystals (Chart 25)

**ENDING AND NEW
BEGINNING CHARTS**

Stages of Grief and Healing (Chart 26)

Letting Go and Death (Chart 27)

Life Transitions (Chart 28)

Gratitude (Chart 29)

Healthy Living (Chart 30)

CHART CATEGORIES

MIND

Limiting Thoughts (Chart 14)

Empowering Thoughts (Chart 15)

EMOTIONS

Feelings (Chart 17)

BODY

Physical Body (Chart 7)

Body Systems (Chart 8)

ENERGY BODY

Energy Body—Auric Layers (Chart 5)

Chakras (Chart 6)

SPIRIT

Seek and Find Spirit (Chart 3)

Spiritual Guides (Chart 4)

HEALING ISSUES

Type of Healing Needed (Chart 9)

Factors Contributing to Disease
   (Chart 10)

Life Stressors (Chart 11)

Addictions (Chart 12)

Blocks to Healing (Chart 13)

Limiting Thoughts (Chart 14)

SOLUTIONS

Yes/No and Clearing Signal (Chart 1)

Time and Percent (Chart 2)

Empowering Thoughts (Chart 15)

Clearing Needed (Chart 16)

Human Needs (Chart 18)

Self-Care (Chart 19)

Healing Arts (Chart 20)

Food (Chart 21)

Vitamins and Minerals (Chart 22)

Flower Essences (Chart 23)

Aromatherapy (Chart 24)

Crystals (Chart 25)

Gratitude (Chart 29)

Healthy Living (Chart 30)

GRIEF

Stages of Grief and Healing (Chart 26)

Letting Go and Death (Chart 27)

Life Transitions (Chart 28)

PREFACE

The Healing Promise

A moment of crisis can be a moment of growth,
as the wounded self prepares to transform. From
the chrysalis of my pain, I will forge my healing—
the wings of my newborn self.

—MARIANNE WILLIAMSON,
A Year of Miracles: Daily Devotions and Reflections

At one time or another, we all have had healing challenges. It's a fundamental aspect of the human journey. If you are like me, as soon as I realize something is wrong, I immediately want to get excellent help and care. In the past, most of us have gone to a Western medical doctor to be examined and most likely been given a prescription or had surgery.

Fortunately, in recent years many complementary and alternative healing methods have become available.[1] Some have come from the East, such as acupuncture, Reiki, and Ayurvedic healing. Some approaches have come from the West, such as chiropractic and naturopathic medicine. These choices emphasize a more holistic methodology that recognizes a person is a whole being with emotional, mental, spiritual, and physical issues. To heal fully, all aspects of the self must be addressed.

---

[1] If a non-mainstream practice is used together with conventional medicine, it's considered "complementary." If a non-mainstream practice is used in place of conventional medicine, it's considered "alternative." National Center for Complementary and Integrated Health (https://nccih.nih.gov/health/integrative-health).

As children, we were not surprised when we skinned our knees and within a few days our bodies had healed. Our bodies continually and automatically balance and heal us in every moment of our lives. Repair happens even when we sleep at night.

We inhabit our bodies and have some awareness, consciously or not, of our own body and its needs. As Lissa Rankin, MD, says in her best-selling book, *Mind Over Medicine*, "After all, who knows the patient's body better than the patient?"[2] By learning to consciously align with our own inner self, we can help ourselves heal.

Remember that our bodies are self-healing beings.

Each of us is unique with complex and different needs. What works for one person may not work for another. *The Book of Pendulum Healing* will assist you in discovering what works best for you in order to help you become a stronger, healthier person. I have outlined for you the step-by-step Intuitive Pendulum Healing Process:

1. Attune to Spirit through prayer or meditation.

2. Learn to dowse with a pendulum.

3. Research using the pendulum with the Intuitive Healing Charts.

4. Clear negative energy and replace with positive energy.

5. Create an Intuitive Healing Action Plan.

6. Transform with Spirit's help the mind, emotions, and spirit.

[2] Lissa Rankin, *Mind Over Medicine* (Carlsbad, CA: Hay House, Inc., 2013), 161–62.

HOW THE BOOK IS ORGANIZED

The Intuitive Pendulum Healing method is simple yet profound and is structured to help you begin to experience dowsing with a pendulum and the Intuitive Healing Charts for yourself.

Divining with a Pendulum, Intuition, and Healing (Chapter 1) introduces pendulum dowsing (also called divining)—an ancient, intuitive art that helps people discover their own truth about themselves.

A Brief History of Dowsing (Chapter 2) explores the fascinating history of dowsing, along with the dowsers who researched, experimented, and utilized the rod and pendulum.

Pendulum and Intuitive Healing Charts Instructions (Chapter 3) opens our minds and center to prepare for pendulum dowsing. We use a "beginner's mind" and take simple steps on our dowsing/divining journey. You will learn how to easily use the pendulum and receive *yes* or *no* answers and how to clear. Clearing with the pendulum is a way to lighten a person, a group of people, and the world of old emotional and mental patterns.

Foundation Charts (Chapter 4) are the basic charts that help with all the other charts.

In **The Arduous Path—The Challenge Charts (Chapter 5)**, we research our spiritual, mental, and physical issues.

Many Paths to Healing—The Solutions Charts (Chapter 6) are designed to give you both traditional and complementary choices. Often, when ill, we feel the world closing in and we succumb to our illnesses. In fact, we do have healthy choices and healing alternatives. Each of us is unique, so we use the charts to find out what combination of treatments will work for us.

In **Transitions, Endings, and New Beginnings Charts (Chapter 7)**, we face transition, death, and the process of rebuilding our lives anew.

Other Pendulum Exercises (Chapter 8) is an exciting chapter in which you put to use your new pendulum and Intuitive Healing Charts skills to communicate with angels and deceased loved ones, and delve deeper into your past lives and the past lives with others.

Other Intuitive Tools for Healing and Connecting with Spirit (Chapter 9) reacquaints and introduces you to time-honored tools—prayer and meditation plus additional tools to help you increase your intuitive powers.

In **Give the Gift of an Intuitive Healing (Chapter 10)**, you will learn to give yourself and others intuitive readings and healings through a step-by-step process.

In **Write Your Own Intuitive Healing Plan (Chapter 11)**, you will take your health into your own hands and be empowered to create an Intuitive Healing Plan.

In **Create a Sacred Healing Circle (Chapter 12)**, you will be inspired to work with others on your healing journey! This chapter offers simple guidelines for starting your own group.

In **Appendix—The Intuitive Healing Charts**, the charts to be used with pendulum dowsing are conveniently located for your exploration.

I promise that most people can learn the methods presented here with practice and persistence. As your intuition is heightened, you will begin to know and trust what is best for your health and life. By seeking inner guidance and making good choices, you can improve your physical, emotional, mental, and spiritual health.

NOTES

I refer to "healing" throughout this book. I am not speaking about "curing," which is the realm of physicians and other health professionals. If clients have a physical problem, I always refer them to medical doctors or other professionals. I believe spiritual or psychic healing can affect the physical healing, but it is not a replacement for the medical profession.

I use the words *divining* and *dowsing* interchangeably throughout the book.

I also use the terms *Higher Power, God, Goddess,* and *Spirit* interchangeably to denote the Great Creator, the Source of All, who in truth is unnameable. There are many other names for God. Please feel comfortable replacing your own name for God as you read this book.

I asked and received clients' permission to write about their wonderful and profound stories. I have changed their names and a few details out of respect for their privacy.

Pendulum divining is simple, elegant, and it works.
Open to your intuitive mind, and discover your own truth.

INTRODUCTION

How I Became a Diviner and Spiritual Healer

Live your life from your heart.
Share from your heart.
And your story will touch and heal people's souls.

—MELODY BEATTIE

I was not born a psychic but a "sensitive" who naturally knew what people were feeling. My mother sometimes scolded me for my insights saying, "You shouldn't talk with adults in such a frank way." But Mom was intuitive herself and told me and my sisters that she had eyes in the back of her head. One of my happiest memories took place at the Japanese Tea Garden in San Francisco's Golden Gate Park when my mother read our tea leaves. My father too had a built-in "truth meter," which made it very difficult to lie in our family.

We were raised in both the Baptist and Lutheran churches. My overly solemn and strict grandfather, Papa John, who should have been a minister, was the one who took all the grandchildren to church on Sundays and to the Bible bookstore afterwards for a small present. When I was twelve, and my grandmother, Nanny, was dying of cancer, my mother angrily complained that my grandfather was never home but instead was off helping build another church. I was shocked that my grandfather would desert my grandmother at such a time. It was not until after my own husband's death that I understood how hard an illness can be on family members. I was able to forgive my grandfather for not being with my grandmother during her last difficult days.

After Nanny's death, I asked many questions, but no one—not my grandfather, nor camp counselors at Christian camps, nor ministers at my church—had any real answers for me. When they couldn't answer my basic question, "Why did God give my grandmother cancer?" and told me instead to have "faith," I stopped believing in a Christian God. How could I believe in a God that took my sweet grandmother in such a painful way?

While attending college, I got married at the young age of nineteen. I had been told that women were supposed to go to college to find a husband. I did! He was smart, generous, older—an attorney, who liked flying kites on green hillsides in Marin and reading science fiction more than practicing law.

At twenty, I read *Seth Speaks* by Jane Roberts. Because I felt so in tune with the concepts that I read about, I read all the Seth books. I also began reading other books about psychic experiences. I took my first meditation class at the local junior college and sat in a hard chair while we meditated as a group.

A few years later, I participated in a paid experiment to sit in a sensory deprivation tank, a float tank—a dark, soundproof container filled with salt water maintained at skin temperature. After an hour of quiet and itching from the salt solution, I realized that I desperately needed to go to counseling, as my marriage was faltering and I was drinking too much.

By the age of twenty-seven with a teaching credential and a degree in anthropology from a small college in the San Joaquin Valley, I left my husband. I moved to San Francisco and began to reshape my life with help from my sister, Therese. We took early Saturday morning kundalini yoga classes. At the end of each class, our teacher played us melodious guitar music—opening my heart and mind to new realities. I also began weekly counseling with a kind, practical man, named Michael, who listened and encouraged me in my new life.

At night, Therese and I experimented with the Ouija board, automatic handwriting, and tarot cards. My newest boyfriend called me a witch. However, on Saturday nights, we were out enjoying the nightlife of North Beach and the Marina, still drinking too much.

I experienced a turning point during a psychic healing class. I learned to feel and balance auras and chakras of others with my hands. I learned about spiritual forces. One night our teacher called in the energy of Jesus. Even though I had been raised in a Christian home, this was my first experience with feeling Jesus's love. Today, I acknowledge he was once the most powerful healer on earth. I still use some of the techniques learned in that first psychic healing class because they were meaningful and still work for me.

In the fall of 1979, I landed my first teaching job working with the most difficult, troubled children in San Francisco. In that first year, I didn't feel I accomplished much, but in the spring, one child, Cesar, finally learned to read. In February of 1980, on a whim I interviewed for a teaching job at Graded School in Sao Paulo, Brazil, where my adventuresome twin sister, Laurie, taught. I got a call on my birthday in March and accepted the position. By July, I was off for a new challenge, a better school, and more opportunity to travel.

While I was overseas, my drinking increased. Outside of school, I had a number of painful, humiliating, and degrading experiences in Sao Paulo. Perhaps it was the pressure of living in a foreign country with a new demanding job. More likely, it was just the natural progression of the disease of alcoholism that runs in my family. When I returned home for the summer, my drinking was even more out of control. I asked both my sisters, Laurie and Therese, to take me to an Alcoholics Anonymous meeting. Funny, I knew just where to go when the time came.

JUST IN TIME

By the time I found Alcoholics Anonymous, I knew I had a frightening relationship with alcohol. I could no longer control my drinking. It controlled me. Through another counselor, not my sisters, I arrived at my first A.A. meeting, wanting to connect with spiritual, preferably like-minded people, who could help me. Looking back, miraculously, I did find a powerful program and spiritual women who were working the Twelve Steps and searching for a Higher Power, A.A.'s name for an all-encompassing, loving Spirit.

At that first meeting, one woman was sharing her story with lightness and a sense of humor. She was a petite, feisty woman, who formerly played and sang at piano bars. She had come to A.A. just six months before, after many long years of drinking. She became my sponsor and, for the next six weeks, saved my life daily. She helped this very sick woman, me, learn to live life one day at a time without alcohol.

During those initial few weeks, after working the first three steps in A.A., I had a spiritual awakening. I felt different . . . lighter, and I had hope I could truly recover. Suddenly, I wanted to know more about my Higher Power. I received two gifts from my girlfriend who sent me the little book by Gerald Jampolsky, *Love Is Letting Go of Fear*, and the Unity publication, "The Daily Word," both of which greatly influenced my future spiritual path.

HOW I MET HIM

A few years later, I met my husband, James Staffen, in a hatha yoga class in Nevada City, California. Our first conversation went something like this:

Me: Yes, I do healing work—massage. And you?

James: Acupressure. I just finished up a powerful class. Do you go to church?

Me: Yes, I belong to the Unity Church, and I'm in A Course in Miracles program. How about you?

James: I'm a Waldorf teacher applying for the Christian Community Ministerial Program.

Me: Great. Any chance you're on the Program? A.A.?

James: Yes.

Me: Where do you go to meetings? At the church?

James: Have I seen you jogging along the Old Highway in the mornings?

Me: Yes, that's me.

James: Could I have your phone number?

He didn't call, but I ran into him at the mini-mart where we both had a yen for the Otis Spunkmeyer chocolate chip cookies—a steal at three for a dollar. He asked me again for my phone number. Months later, we married, eventually had two children, and ran a high tech marketing company—a story for another day.

Together we created a wonderful life in a small, old-fashioned lumber town in the Santa Cruz Mountains in Boulder Creek, California. Our children were in elementary school, and we had our challenges like most young couples, being stretched between work and home duties—too little money at times and too little time to fit everything in. But it was a holy, sweet life, and I remember thinking six months before James got sick, "I should be very grateful."

MY DARK NIGHT OF THE SOUL

Seemingly out of nowhere James had a seizure and was diagnosed with brain cancer. He was forty-seven. A cloud of darkness truly seemed to prevail over our house and our little family of four, which included our children—Adam, nine, and Danielle, seven. The movie *Independence Day* came out around that time. In one scene in the movie, the spaceship from above casts a giant shadow over the city. That's how it felt. A dark shadow descended on our house. I was very angry with God/Goddess. How could this happen and why?

In many ways I was fortunate because I had so much help from friends, many saying healing prayers for us. I had sweet sisters who were there for my husband's operations and later the trip to Texas for alternative treatment. We had supportive neighbors; one was a nurse who worked at our local hospital, and the other a wonderful doctor who told us we could come to his house any time for help.

Throughout James's illness, even though I was angry with God, I still believed in the angels and called on them often. I talked to them in my journal, and they always told me the truth: "He will not live." But they counseled me to live in the present, to enjoy the small miracles of everyday life, and to treasure the moments we had together.

Between operations and treatments, when James was feeling up to it, we took trips to places we had loved, sometimes as a couple, sometimes as a family. We found natural beauty to be so healing in Big Sur, Calistoga, Lake Tahoe, and Hawaii. Near the end, James and I cruised to Alaska, where loving people treated us kindly and where we forgot for a while about our dire situation.

Really, I don't know how I did it, except I know it was the angels who carried me. They held me and helped me sleep at night, got me up in the morning, helped me take care of James, drive the kids to school, and take myself off to work. One huge blessing was that James's best friend, who had survived cancer, took care of James during the day.

Holding our work life together was left to me. Two sales employees plotted ways in which to take over our company. I had to fire them and find a new sales team. Later, I would be criticized for focusing on the business, as my husband grew more ill. But of course, it paid all the bills—the health insurance, the extra medical costs, help in the home, the mortgage, and food for the table. Thank God. We had created it together. It sustained us through the dark times.

At the end of James's life, the doctors tried their best to "save" my husband over and over again, but then I felt he became their experiment, rather than a human being. I knew that the cancer treatments were awful—they just made him sick, and there came a point when we were all exhausted. We hoped for the best but had little faith. Not even the doctors believed the chemotherapy they prescribed would work.

Slowly, James was leaving us, and he began to seem like a stranger.

All of those who had supported us through the ordeal were with him in the last moments of his life at Dominican Hospital in Santa Cruz. For three precious days, we had flowers, prayer circles, harp and flute music, and three different ministers visiting. We entered a new dimension, where it felt as though the angels and Spirit were present. We experienced a deep peace as James let go and left his body.

While grieving during the months that followed, I experienced again the difficult lesson of surrender and acceptance, both of which I learned so well from A.A. Surrender—don't fight what is happening. Surrender—know there is a higher purpose, even if in the depths of despair you cannot fathom why or what happened. As for the gift of acceptance— you don't have to like it, you can hate it, but "accept the things you cannot change" as taught in the Serenity Prayer.

Even after counseling by myself and with my children, with kind, understanding, and wise therapists, I felt I still was not whole. It seemed as if my will to go on and my joy for living were pieces that were lost. I was now the sole owner of our business and a single parent. I didn't know how I would manage this new life.

HOW I WAS INTRODUCED TO DOWSING AND A SPIRITUAL HEALER

One day I found Spiritual Response Therapy (SRT),[3] or it found me. A woman at work told me about this amazing woman, Shakti Wilson, the wife of the new minister at the Unity Church, who was giving a workshop at church the next Saturday. As I experienced the SRT process of being counseled and healed, I immediately felt a kinship and understood the power of the pendulum and SRT Charts.

[3] Spiritual Response Therapy is a spiritual-energetic approach to clearing the template of the body upon which the physical, mental, and emotional health depends. The work is done in an altered state, using a pendulum and a set of charts.

I began to learn the process of using a pendulum to clear, charts to research, and the way prayer heals. I could do all this in the quiet and privacy of my own home. It was safe, and I could go at my own pace. Over the days and months, I cleared the deep grief about my late husband and the grief about my life, as well as lifetimes of karma. SRT healed the energetic hole in my heart and soul, bringing the light in again and giving me a way back to God/Goddess.

It was a fascinating experience—truly talking with the cosmos. I began having my own knowledge and familiarity of those on the other side. In addition, I had experiences with Mary Magdalene, Jesus, Myrtle Fillmore (cofounder of Unity Church), and the angels of light and love. SRT changed my ideas of life and death. I felt I was being guided and taught by wise spiritual guides on the other side—all done in a quiet way after I put my children to bed. After three years of counseling, coaching, and taking classes, I became certified in SRT, and I began to give readings and healings.

I had many encounters with my late husband after he died. I dreamed that he visited and sat in my chair in my bedroom. It felt like him because he very seriously asked me to please hang up my clothes so he would have a place to sit. Isn't that funny? After the dream, I always kept the chair cleared of my things and left him little food presents on the table next to the chair.

It took me years to emotionally realize that the difficult and dark times I traveled through with my husband, James, friends, and family were not retribution. I was not alone, and I was not being punished. This journey was life on life's terms. In the end God/Goddess takes every dark thing to use for good. Out of those times I learned to survive, then recover, and now thrive in the grace of God/Goddess.

My own Intuitive Charts and books, *Divination & Joy* and *Divination & Action*, were borne of the challenges and solutions I was encountering while working with people. In the last few years I created *The Book of Pendulum Healing* and the Intuitive Healing Charts out of a need to help people with their obstacles to health and help them find solutions to their problems.

Through the pendulum and charts, I was even able to help my late husband on the other side after I spontaneously learned how to communicate with deceased loved ones. I would be using my pendulum and charts and suddenly feel James's presence. I realized I could use the charts to ask what he wanted to communicate and to ask what he needed. Also, I communicated with him in my journal pages. I truly learned there is no death of the spirit. Though the bodies of loved ones die, their spirit lives on.

I naturally became closer to my Higher Power and angels. Truly, I was carried. On the other side of death, I found new strength and independence. Through dowsing and divining, I gained a deep understanding of life, and all that it means to be both human and spiritual, living in a mysterious universe.

Today, my children are grown, and I have found a new home living at the Tannery Arts Lofts, an intentional arts community in Santa Cruz, where I write, paint, and give spiritual readings and classes. I feel blessed to have such a rich and fulfilling life.

Now, I'd like to invite you to come join me as we learn about the amazing magic of the pendulum and the Intuitive Healing Charts.

CHAPTER 1

Divining with a Pendulum, Intuition, and Healing

Dowsing is "human communication with the cosmos."

—CHRISTOPHER BIRD, *The Divining Hand*

What if there were a simple tool that could answer truthfully any question we might have? What if this were easy to learn and use? What if this instrument could help us make great decisions about anything in our life? The *pendulum*—a body suspended from a fixed point so as to swing freely to and fro under the action of gravity—is such a tool.

When I first learned to use a pendulum, I didn't know it would take me on a healing journey. I didn't know what "dowsing" was and why it could change my life. I just saw a demonstration, tried it myself, and suddenly I wanted to know everything I could about it. At first, I did not question why it worked; I just accepted the healings I was receiving. When someone throws you a lifeline, you don't question the maker of the rope.

Over time I read, took classes, and became trained in Spiritual Response Therapy (SRT), which utilizes the pendulum and a chart system. Eventually, I became an SRT consultant. I have given spiritual readings and healings now since 2004. The more I work with pendulum dowsing and the Intuitive Charts, the more intrigued I become.

It is important to have background knowledge so you know that what you are learning has been studied, has a long history, and is legitimate. Before we get into the history in the next chapter, I want to share more about what intuitive pendulum healing is and is not. Let's start with the subject of dowsing.

To *dowse*, the more scientific term, means to *search* with a rod or pendulum for anything. A sister word, more spiritual, is to *divine*, to discover by intuition, the direct knowing of truth. In this book, I use both terms interchangeably. In this and the last century, dowsing (or divining) has gone through a paradigm shift.

Once used primarily for finding water or minerals, today dowsing is used to search for and understand the mysteries of earth, spirit, and healing. In her book *Dowsing, the Ultimate Guide for the 21st Century*, Elizabeth Brown, a dowser in Britain, describes dowsing as "a way of finding out by accessing information with direct intent, using a means outside the five senses and culminating in a physical response within the human body."[4]

Dowsing is an art form, rather than a science. After centuries of study, it hasn't yet been adequately explained. But we know through empirical evidence that it works. Two primary types of dowsing are *field dowsing* for resources and *information dowsing* for remote information.

Field dowsing is the form that is most well known. You might have seen pictures of an older gentleman holding a rod or forked willow branch in both hands in front of him and slowly walking across a field to find water or resources. This is field dowsing.

Information dowsing is analogous to remote viewing, which can be done using maps, charts, or simply by asking *yes* or *no* questions. Russell Targ, a physicist and researcher at Stanford Research Institute for two decades, documented in repeated experiments that humans have the capacity to perceive and describe scenes remotely and that these psychic

[4] Elizabeth Brown, *Dowsing, the Ultimate Guide for the 21st Century* (London, England and Carlsbad, CA: Hay House, 2010), 4.

abilities are real. As Targ says in his book *Limitless Mind*, "Remote viewing is an example of nonlocal ability. It has repeatedly allowed people to describe, draw, and experience objects and activities anywhere on the planet, contemporaneously or in the near future."[5]

How does it work? The dowser projects an intent, a request for information, and through the mind of the dowser and an instrument (a rod or a pendulum), an answer is fed back. The dowser picks up a signal. It's a type of clairvoyance, seeing beyond the ordinary. We might compare it to making a phone call; if we dial correctly, we get the right person, or in more modern terms, we ask a question of Google and we receive an answer back. However, in the case of dowsing, we are connecting with the collective unconsciousness. Just as animals home in on targets and mysteriously find their way home if lost, we humans have the capacity through intention, practice, and dowsing—by using all our innate senses—to seek and find our truth.

When dowsing, we are using our mind, body, and spirit, and a pendulum to access the invisible realm. With practice and through study of the pendulum and the Intuitive Healing Charts, we have a practical yet profound way to access the spiritual world. When we use the pendulum, the innate intuitive self will be automatically activated. With the help of our super-consciousness, we will be guided to understand both the problems and the solutions available. The pendulum acts as a compass, the charts as a map. You can then create your own healing plan.

I read from Deepak Chopra's book *Reinventing the Body, Resurrecting the Soul*: "Your body is the juncture between the visible and invisible world."[6] Just as our energy body and chakras are our link within our body to the physical and nonphysical aspects of our bodies, so the body is a link between material and spiritual worlds.

[5] Russell Targ, *Limitless Mind: A Guide to Remote Viewing and Transformation of Consciousness* (Novato, CA: New World Library, 2004), xxviii.

[6] Deepak Chopra, *Reinventing the Body, Resurrecting the Soul* (New York, NY: Three Rivers Press, 2009), 21.

Should we become sick, it's wise to look at all aspects of our being. Yes, most assuredly, go to the doctor, especially when facing imminent danger, but also do the inner work (afterwards) to discover the bigger picture, finding out what is out of balance—spiritually, mentally, and emotionally.

We may have this inner realization that we are not just a physical being, but energetic, spiritual beings as well. That we are not just this lump of flesh, but made of light. Not just physical machines with various parts that break and are fixed or not, but in the words of Father Teilhard de Chardin, "We are spiritual beings having a human experience."[7] With the pendulum and the Intuitive Healing Charts, we can begin investigating, learning, and truly healing; and in the process we can come to know ourselves at a much deeper level.

Because we live in a materialistic society, we must actively seek and find our connection with the spirit within and without, the greatest earthly gift we can have. When we discover our true nature, it is important to create a daily practice to nurture and enhance this most necessary connection, to survive and thrive on earth. We each find our own way, in our own time, on our individual, earthly, and spiritual path: practicing yoga, meditating, dowsing with a pendulum, reading, spending time in nature, riding a bike, jogging, working in Artist Way Groups, taking part in twelve-step programs, studying *A Course in Miracles*, and yes, observing traditional and nontraditional religions.

As we connect with Spirit and dowse, we activate our intuition, our direct knowledge of the truth and a natural part of our human make-up. Intuition bypasses the rational mind, gives us quick solutions necessary for survival and for living a good life in the present. Children use this sixth sense, but then are taught to think more logically and distrust it. So by the time most of us grow up, we have learned to ignore our intuition and our bodies, and with that, our health, to our own detriment.

. . . .

[7] See https://www.brainyquote.com/quotes/pierre_teilhard_de_chardi_160888.

The good news is that when we combine our innate intuition with divining and the Intuitive Healing Charts, we receive guidance from our High Self. The more we practice, the more intuitive we become. Some of us even become psychics or spiritual healers.

In addition, dowsing with our intuitive senses awakened is a magic key to living a better life. In our information-rich world, we can find the facts, which are frequently contradictory, but we often don't know what is best for us. Dowsing guides us to what will help us. We are drawing from both inner wisdom and outer spiritual guidance, taking many factors into consideration of which we might not be aware. If it just doesn't feel right, we look further for information. An intuitive insight comes quickly, so we can take immediate action. This can save us.

There can be a deep fear about knowing ourselves. We might believe or feel deep within that we are not worthy of God or of healing. I had this feeling when I first got sober. I felt so bad about myself, so lost and separate from God/Goddess, I did not believe They could love me.

There is the flip side of the coin too: we fear our greatness. As Marianne Williamson so eloquently said, "Our deepest fear is not that we are inadequate. Our deepest fear is that we are powerful beyond measure. It is our Light, not our Darkness, that most frightens us."[8]

The Intuitive Healing Charts can be used on many different levels. First, on a physical level, the charts can be used to maintain our health. Second, the charts can help us when we are out of balance mentally or emotionally. The charts can point us in the right direction as to what forms of self-care would be best to regain equilibrium. And when we become sick, by using the charts, we can decide what professional help would be best for us. Should we have an ongoing condition, we can learn what could be nurturing and sustaining to our health. We can find self-care and healing arts solutions, so we can reduce the amount of medical care we need. Also, the Chart System ultimately encourages us to

---

[8] Marianne Williams, *A Return to Love: Reflections on the Principles of "A Course in Miracles"* (New York, NY: HarperCollins, 1993), 190.

develop good habits, to get plenty of rest, eat well, find healthy exercise, and have fun.

By using this healing system, we can learn to cultivate awareness and listen to our mind-body-spirit self, discovering what we truly need. Many questions can arise: Are we taking care of all aspects of ourselves? Is there a practice that would be helpful for our spiritual development? Are we eating the right foods, getting enough exercise, and drinking enough water? Are we in the right career? Living in the right place? In a relationship with the right person or people? Or do we have to make changes?

We may be commuting long distances to our jobs, working extended hours, sitting at a computer screen all day with only short breaks. Some of us have lived the crazy, modern life, always achieving, rather than being, forgetting our families and our deeper selves, just so we can get ahead.

I had my moments of clarity—sitting in front of my computer at work. It felt as if I had a mind freeze for two or three seconds. I never went to a doctor, but it was a sign to me I needed to make some radical changes. Then it happened again a month later, and I did take action. Though scared to reorganize my company because of the financial hit I knew I would take, I realized I needed to transition. A few months later, I right-sized my company and created a smaller office in my hometown, and my employees became my contractors. I was happier, and so were they, working from home and well paid.

Remember, healing is a process that can often take time. The disease was not created overnight, and sometimes the healing will take time too. Patience. Oh, I hate that word. But I have learned to remind myself that God/Goddess works in mysterious ways. When I align myself with Spirit, all things are possible. Even me, being patient with my body, as it heals.

So what is *intuitive pendulum healing*? It is a system whereby you will have a process to discover your health challenges and potential solutions and make powerful, strong decisions for yourself. You will also observe that you are quite naturally becoming more intuitive, receiving information fluidly from a higher source with the flow unblocked and open. This process can take from a month or a few months to a year.

This is the beginning of the journey, where you can find some powerful answers, but not all. Keep searching for yourself until you find all that can heal you.

Thus, healing of the body, mind, and spirit leads us back to the mystery of the Self—who we have always been and always will be—that part of us that inhabits a body but leaves when the journey is over.

SEVEN REASONS YOU SHOULD LEARN TO USE A PENDULUM AND THE INTUITIVE HEALING CHARTS

1. Learning and practicing the pendulum will help you make wiser decisions for your health and life.

2. As you make life-affirming decisions for yourself, you will feel better mentally, emotionally, and spiritually.

3. By doing the exercises throughout the book, you will have a better relationship with yourself and your body.

4. When you take the time to center, ground, and use your pendulum, you will find you are naturally connected to a Higher Power.

5. Pendulum dowsing is both practical and spiritual and will take you on a mystical journey.

6. Your intuition will expand and flow into every part of your life.

7. Your creativity and imagination will flourish.

Next, we will delve into the history of dowsing with rods and pendulum. Or, if you want, you can skip ahead and first experiment with the pendulum and the charts. You might just want to get down to the business of dowsing and begin your discovery and healing process.

CHAPTER 2

A Brief History of Dowsing

Dowsing was revealing the divine in man.

—CHRISTOPHER BIRD, *The Divining Hand*

Researching dowsing history has been fascinating for me, yet this is but a brief look into that vast past. For a more complete and detailed history, please see *The Divining Hand* by Christopher Bird. I bought my used copy on Amazon and was so pleased to see the author, now deceased, had signed the book. The signed copy made me feel as if he were personally giving his book to me. The inscription said "to June" and here I am in June writing my book, and using his book for research—a sweet synchronicity.

Dowsing has been used for centuries, first by shamans and tribal leaders. But the first reliable evidence of dowsing is found in bas-reliefs from ancient Egypt portraying water dowsers with rods. Dowsing was also utilized to determine the best places to grow crops. Diviners in China also used rod-like tools to find water beneath the ground. An emperor, Ta Yu, born in 2205 BCE was known for finding subterranean water. In a Chinese bas-relief, he is shown holding a branched rod, like a tuning fork.

The Bible reports that Moses used a rod to strike for water. But later, in Roman times, a person could be condemned to death for using the pendulum. In 1326, Pope John XXII banned the "use of a ring to obtain answers," an early form of pendulum dowsing to determine the sex of an unborn child.

Over the past eight hundred years, dowsing both gained and lost respectability and popularity while it continued being used, studied, and investigated by German, French, and British scientists and engineers. They gathered much empirical evidence showing that dowsing works for finding water, oil, and minerals. But, after centuries of research, they were unable to scientifically understand exactly how or why dowsing works. Today it is still a mystery, an unexplainable fact.

From the thirteenth century on, dowsing in Germany was used to find mineral ores, as well as water. *The Nature of Minerals*, the first book that discusses dowsing extensively, was originally published in 1556, one year after the death of its author, Georg Bauer, who is also known as Georgius Agricola. The book contains captivating woodcuts illustrating dowsing methods.

In the mid 1500s, Queen Elizabeth I, eager to keep pace with technological growth and mining wealth in the German lands, invited miners and dowsers to England to introduce mineral dowsing and mining to England. By the 1700s and 1800s, in England, France, and in the German lands, many books on mining and engineering included information about dowsing.

Today, in Germany, in museums of natural history, science, mining, and engineering, and in private collections of art and sculpture, there are displays of woodcarvings, paintings, and drawings featuring dowsers holding forked sticks.

Ironically, in the seventeenth and eighteenth centuries, both Catholic and Protestant churches condemned dowsing, but many of the clergy were active dowsers. By the early twentieth century, four pioneering priests who were intrigued by dowsing subsequently opened up a new field—medical dowsing.

THE PRIESTLY BEGINNINGS OF MEDICAL DOWSING

Abbé Alexis-Timothée Bouly, a master dowser, was able to locate water in France and across Europe. After World War I, a general heard of his skills and called upon him to locate unexploded shells. After the war,

Bouly created the Society of Friends of Radiesthesia. (*Radiesthesia* was his new word for dowsing.) He specialized in the research of health and microbes. In his later life, in 1950, he was knighted and made a *Chevalier de la Legion d'Honneur*, France's highest honor.

A second priest, Abbé Alexis Mermet, who lived at the turn of the twentieth century, was taught by his father to dowse. Talented with the pendulum, he came to the conclusion that one could use a pendulum not only to discover what was in the earth but also to discover hidden conditions in human beings and animals. He published his findings in the book *How I Proceeded in the Discovery of Near or Distant Water, Metals, Hidden Objects and Illnesses*. In addition to healing people and animals, he helped find water in South America using a map and remote viewing. He was helpful with finding missing people and animals anywhere in the world. He also assisted with archeology research in Rome, and the Vatican later recognized him for his remarkable ability with the pendulum.

A third priest, Father Jean-Louis Bourdoux, worked as a missionary-priest in the jungles of Brazil for sixteen years. He became quite ill and almost died from consumption and fever, but he was given saps from local plants and healed by a medicine man. Later, he began studying Amazonian plants, which he brought back to France, where they were tested by homeopaths. Bourdoux also wanted a way to help other missionaries discover what would help them when they were far from home. Inspired by the Abbé Mermet, Bourdoux learned to dowse. He returned to South America, and after years of study, he wrote his book, *Practical Notions of Radiesthesia for Missionaries*.

After World War II, a fourth priest, Father Jean Jurion, learned of and studied the dowsing methods used by Bouly, Bourdoux, and Mermet. He began working with patients that other medical doctors had given up on—using the pendulum and homeopathy. As his success grew, the French medical establishment became upset with him because, although he did not have a medical degree, he achieved excellent results. He was taken to court ten times, but he continued to follow Christ's admonition to "heal the sick." Jurion treated thirty thousand patients over a thirty-year span, diagnosing with the pendulum and treating his patients with homeopathy. He left thirty thousand medical records and a 2,000-page treatise on homeopathy. He observed that "in countries such as the Netherlands, Germany and Great Britain, no law forbids doctors from working together with unorthodox healers."[9] Jurion's successes in treating people encouraged other lay people to also "heal the sick."

Jurion founded and was president of the Union of Medical Dowsers. In 1967, with the support of Robert Felsenhardt (a chief executive officer of a French insurance company who was won over by Jurion's success and himself became a dowser), he was instrumental in helping over one hundred medical dowsers to obtain official recognition by the French Ministry of Labor and be allowed to practice their art in France.

DOCTORS IN ENGLAND EXPLORE, RESEARCH, AND USE DOWSING FOR HEALING

Meanwhile in England, a young doctor named Aubrey Westlake had an attack of food poisoning. Traditional doctors were unable to help him. He turned to and was healed by Hector Munro, another doctor who used a laying on of hands to diagnose the problem. After recovering, Westlake asked Munro where he had learned his methods, and Westlake was invited to join the newly formed Medical Society for the Study of Radiesthesia, where he learned much more about this type of healing.

Westlake and his wife (she seemed to be more proficient with a pendulum than her husband) studied dowsing. They realized it was necessary to approach the study of medicine in a totally different way. "The weakness of ordinary medicine," Westlake concluded was that because "it stressed pathology above all else, it dealt mainly with the gross final results of disease process rather than their underlying cause."[10] True

---

[9] Christopher Bird, *The Divining Hand* (New York, NY: E. P. Dutton, 1979), 291.

diagnosis, he felt, was to be sought in a radiesthetic analysis (using the pendulum for diagnosis), not of pathological tissue, but of a harmonious balance of energy patterns constituting health. After years of practice and study he wrote the book *The Pattern of Health*.[11]

And now we take a leap over the pond to the United States.

A SHORT HISTORY OF SPIRITUAL RESPONSE THERAPY

Spiritual Response Therapy is the amazing program where I was initially trained in using the pendulum and a set of thirty-three charts. Grieving over the loss of my husband, James, and searching for healing for my soul, I was fortunate to take classes by Shakti Wilson, a teacher and minister affiliated with the Spiritual Response Association (SRA). As I took the workshops over a period of two years and learned to use the SRT system, I released my negative programming and cleared past life energies along with soul programming. I was so enthusiastic about the growth I achieved that I became an SRA consultant myself.

Robert Detzler, a Unity minister in San Jose, California, and his wife were introduced to sociologist Dr. Clark Cameron's ideas in a six-month training course, and Detzler began using these ideas in his ministerial counseling. When his Board of Directors disapproved, Detzler left the church and devoted himself full time to SRT. Later with his wife, he established a new religious educational organization, the Spiritual Response Association in Washington state.

I was fortunate to meet Robert and his wife, Mary Ann, creators of Spiritual Response Therapy and founders of the Spiritual Response Association, just once, when they were giving an advanced SRT class in

---

[10] Bird, *The Divining Hand*, 291.

[11] Aubrey T. Westlake, *The Pattern of Health* (Berkeley, CA and London, England: Shambhala Publications, Inc., 1974).

Scotts Valley, California. A tall, lanky man, Robert was passionate and opinionated about his work. He was older, strict, and a bit domineering. But Mary Ann complemented her husband perfectly. She was soft-spoken, and her words came from the heart as she explained the SRT work in gentler tones. Her kindness was palpable.

Detzler's books, *The Freedom Path* and *Soul Re-Creation* (among others), have been translated into multiple languages. Today SRA has 140 certified teachers and 125 certified consultants working in 45 countries, as well as 13 ordained ministers worldwide. You can find more information about SRA at *www.spiritualresponse.com*.

Detzler had great success in healing people emotionally and spiritually. Sometimes as a consequence, those clients were also healed physically from chronic conditions such as allergies and asthma.

Because of the efforts of these practitioners, divining with pendulums today is flourishing. Spiritual and Reiki healers use pendulums to clear, balance, and heal their clients. Homeopaths, flower essence practitioners, and aromatherapy practitioners also use the pendulum to find the right remedies for their clients. If you walk into any New Age, spiritual, or crystal store, you will find beautiful pendulums waiting for you.

To find out more about the history of dowsing and current uses, explore the British Society of Dowsers, with 1,600 members, at https://britishdowsers.org and the American Society of Dowsers with 3,000 members at https://dowsers.org.

In the next chapter, you will learn how to use the pendulum and the Intuitive Healing Charts to make superior decisions for your health and well-being.

CHAPTER 3

Pendulum and Intuitive
Healing Charts Instructions

Nature has been generous with the gift of dowsing.

—RAYMOND C. WILLEY, *Modern Dowsing*

In workshops I've given over the years, almost everyone in the class—after only an hour—is able to dowse successfully with a pendulum. I am amazed at most people's abilities to divine with a pendulum, and I love seeing the light come into people's eyes when they see—*yes, yes*—they too can dowse.

As you read on, imagine that I am right here with you giving you encouragement. Know that Spirit wants to connect with you and wants you to learn to dowse. God/Goddess's will for you is that you will be able to divine and be completely healthy.

Recently, I had the pleasure of working with a new pendulum user. She had never dowsed before. First, I led her in a grounding meditation in which we connected to angels and Spirit and reviewed the pendulum and chart instructions. She then held her pendulum between her thumb and index finger, and as I sat next to her, for the first time, we both saw her pendulum move without her conscious volition.

"Oh my gosh. It moved. I wasn't moving it. Look, it's moving." Then she asked, "What's making it move?"

Then my client and I practiced asking and receiving answers to *yes* and *no* questions to train her pendulum. First, the questions are simple;

for instance, "Is my cat's name _____?" or "Am I ____ years old?" or "My name is _____."

Then she asked, "But how does it work?"

This is the mystery that scientists have been studying for centuries. When you use the pendulum, you are not consciously moving your fingers, hand, or wrist, and it appears that the pendulum is moving on its own. This is called the "ideomotor response." The pendulum is responding to our subconscious and super-conscious messages through our subtle body movements. When we are connected with our Higher Power and angels, they can also influence the pendulum.

I explained to her that after we clear and ask a question, we tap into both our subconscious and super-conscious minds. When we ask about something or someone outside of ourselves, we are sending out a request to the universal consciousness. The pendulum acts as an antenna to receive information, and the mind becomes the receiving instrument.

Then my client wanted to jump right to the Intuitive Healing Charts for more in-depth questions and answers. When we learn how to use the pendulum with the charts, it's as if we've gone from a binary *yes* and *no* system to a multi-choice system. This is the juicy stuff.

When I first learned to use a pendulum, I was fortunate—it felt natural. My mind was open to the experience, and I just followed the simple instructions. I began practicing in the one-hour class and later at home. I asked questions and more questions about my life to test it. Over the days and weeks, I found myself depending on the pendulum for making small decisions, and later I asked bigger questions as I trusted the answers I was given.

The act of using the pendulum with the charts and asking questions and receiving answers is a shortcut for making decisions and understanding challenges. Time can be reduced between comprehending a problem and finding a wise solution to whatever dilemma presents itself. Also, the pendulum can help us to center emotionally. After pendulum dowsing and clearing, we can more easily open to a meditative state, where we become calm, relaxed, and receptive to the suggestions presented by the pendulum and charts.

When beginning to use the pendulum, let yourself approach this new skill with childlike wonder and awe. If you are skeptical, just remember you were a child once. Children have a much easier time learning because they have no preconceived notions of what is possible and what is not. So, find the curious child within and give yourself the gift of patience with yourself and the pendulum.

Just as with any talent or skill, some will be able to use the pendulum more easily, and for others, it will take longer. We all have different experiences, but I guarantee that if you loosen up and give yourself time, you will be able to use the pendulum. As my friend Susan says, "It is so easy to use, it's surprising."

Later in this chapter you will learn to prepare for dowsing by doing a centering or grounding meditation; then I'll teach you how to use the pendulum; and finally, you will learn how to use the pendulum with the charts. Yes, you too can, with patience and an open mind, learn to dowse.

ALL ABOUT PENDULUMS

Pendulums in dowsing are used primarily to gather information or answer questions about anything. For example, we can ask any *yes* and *no* questions. An example would be to find out which vitamins or herbs are best for our bodies. Or we can use the pendulum with the Intuitive Healing Charts to ask and answer numerous questions about our health.

You might already know what a pendulum is—a small weight suspended on a chain that can move to and fro. You might have seen them in spiritual bookstores or in crystal stores. You might have been attracted to them but not understood how they could be used.

Pendulums come in all sizes and weights. A French Catholic priest, Father Jean Jurion, introduced in Chapter 2, famous for his healing practice using pendulums and homeopathy, tried several hundred pendulums of all kinds, shapes, and sizes. He found that most pendulums worked in a similar fashion, so he chose a simple translucent, beautiful crystal for his practice.

I intuitively feel that pendulums have their own little personalities. Depending on the stone, the chain, and any other charms that are
attached, they emit different frequencies. When I go into my little spiritual store and stand in front of the case where the pendulums are hanging, many of them will start moving. They are always saying to me, "Buy
me. Take me home. I will be a great pendulum for you."

A funny little story: I have a girlfriend who loves pendulums. She
took her favorite one to a crystal store, and her pendulum picked out
a mate for itself. The two pendulums fell in love. Now she keeps them
side-by-side in separate little pouches. Otherwise, they get too tangled.
She brought the two pendulums to class, held them both up, and they
entwined with each other—so sweet.

Purchasing a Pendulum

Once you decide you want a pendulum, you might start seeing them
everywhere—your metaphysical bookstore (online or off), at a jewelry
store, or at a rock or crystal store. Have fun looking and try out different
ones to see what works for you.

The pendulum you are attracted to by color, weight, or materials—
the one that you find aesthetically pleasing—is the best one for you.
At the store, pick out a pendulum that you like and see how it feels
in your hand. You can experiment with them, asking a few simple *yes*
and *no* questions and see if you receive a response; you will know if
the pendulum is a match for you. You can also use a pendulum to find
a second pendulum, or if you are buying one for a friend, ask if it is a
good match.

Some people experiment with a variety of pendulums. They come in
many different materials—from crystal to brass, from wood to glass—
and in different shapes. One French collector has over a thousand. Find
what aesthetically appeals to you. Again, when holding a pendulum,
make sure it feels good in your hand. You may experiment with several
different types.

Making a Pendulum

Even better than purchasing a pendulum—you can create your own. We did this in my class, and I was so amazed by my students' creativity. We had so much fun. You might want to use a pendant and chain from your own jewelry box or find a pointed object that can be hung on a string, such as a crystal, gem, or stone. Attach it to a four- to five-inch string, a silver or gold chain, or silk cord if you prefer. The weight of the pendulum should be in proportion to the weight of the chain or string so that they are in balance with each other. For instance, you would want to use a heavy chain with a larger pendant. Remember that the pendulum must swing to and fro unencumbered and you should feel comfortable using it.

THE RIGHT TIME TO DOWSE

When is the right time to dowse? Any time!

But my favorite time to dowse is in the morning after meditation. I find that if I've had a good night's sleep, I am naturally in tune with Spirit. If I don't have to rush off for an appointment and I have time to truly relax and give myself the experience, then I feel my answers are clearer.

Dowsing is an art, and some days we might feel more the presence of our High Self and Higher Power. If I'm grouchy or irritated from too little sleep, I may need to take a bit more time to clear, center, and ground.

Sometimes just picking up the pendulum when upset can be very comforting. It's an outer sign that we are attempting to connect with our High Self and Spirit. The pendulum is a reminder of a spiritual connection that is always there, to which we can become receptive in a moment.

Another little hint—dowsing right before bed can also be nourishing. My girlfriend who is a therapist loves to dowse and clear herself of the day's drama. This allows her to sleep well and have peaceful dreams.

If you are emotionally upset, it's not a good time to dowse. Wait until you feel more yourself and centered, and then work with the pendulum.

SPIRITUAL PREPARATION FOR USING THE CHARTS

We must prepare spiritually for using the Charts to ensure that we are plugged into the highest sources for answers. Just as we need to plug into the correct current of electricity for our appliances and energy needs in our homes and offices, we need to connect with our super-consciousness and Source to dowse. As we become more attuned, over time this process becomes easier and quicker.

Use the centering meditation or the grounding meditation described next. I like to always center before starting, or if I have more time and need, I love spending just a few minutes practicing the grounding meditation too.

Centering Meditation

Take three to five minutes to center yourself before beginning to learn to dowse. It's a good idea to turn off your phone and set a timer. That way you can truly let go.

This is a short meditation to relax and breathe. Doesn't that sound good in your busy day? By centering, we bring our consciousness to our breath, and we attempt to quiet the busy mind. As you take time to do this, your mind will more naturally find its center. Afterwards, you will be ready to use your pendulum, do research, and be prepared to receive correct answers.

Close your eyes and take a few deep breaths. You might want to let out a few sighs or noises ("ah, ah") and let yourself relax. Then, either out loud or to yourself, ask your High Self, your spiritual guide, or Spirit to merge and become present in your mind, heart, and spirit.

As you continue to breathe, consciously lower your shoulders and ask your body to relax. Move your consciousness to your toes and wiggle them. Feel your feet on the ground. Breathe slowly and rhythmically, and feel your chest moving up and down as the air enters and leaves your lungs.

Inwardly say a short, calming, affirmative phrase—for instance, "I am at peace and healing." Or "I am relaxed, ready, and having fun using my pendulum." Repeat the phrase, saying it slowly for three to five minutes.

When your mind meanders off into thoughts or worries, simply bring it back to the breath and affirmation. When your timer rings, give yourself a few seconds, wiggle your toes, stretch, and open your eyes.

Grounding Meditation

For years in my classes and counseling sessions, I've used a grounding meditation. I have found that many of us in contemporary life—including myself—become ungrounded. We are so busy with duties and responsibilities that it's as if we are all operating a few inches or feet off the ground. The meditation that follows allows us to slow down, concentrate on bringing our energy into our bodies and our feet, and connect with the Divine Earth Mother, who provides us with a home and a life.

After all, how can we heal ourselves, if we aren't at home in the body?

Take a moment to get comfortable in your chair. You may want to loosen your shoes or take them off. Place your feet on the ground, and feel them on the floor or carpet. Take a few deep breaths. As you do, begin to notice your breath flowing in and out of your nose. Take a moment to loosen your shoulders, perhaps moving them up and down. You can even sigh and make a little noise to release any frustration you might be feeling. Again, as you breathe in and out, notice the breath moving. You might want to notice how you are feeling. Happy? A little sad? Or angry? While you breathe, just attempt to be with the emotion for a few seconds, and then let the emotion discharge with the breath.

Now, move your consciousness down, down to your feet. Imagine you have little green roots growing from your feet, growing longer and longer. Then traveling at the speed of light in an instant, they connect to the center of the earth. Ask to connect to your Divine Earth Mother. (Every time I do this, I see that Divine Earth Mother has a different costume on, and she likes to celebrate with us. Sometimes too she has a message for me or for the class I am teaching. In your mind's eye, at first you might not see or feel the connection with Divine Earth Mother, but in time as you practice, this will come more easily.)

Now bring up Divine Earth Mother's green and gold energy into your feet. Feel the connection, and bring it into your toes, the soles of your feet, and your ankles, then up into your legs and calves, and into the knees. Visualize the green and gold energy, touching every cell, every ligament, tendon, and bone.

As you remember to breathe slowly, bring the energy further up your legs and into your pelvic region. Send a giant taproot from your first (root) and second (sacral) chakras to the center of the earth connecting with Divine Earth Mother, who gives us her life force. Then bring that green and gold energy up into your pelvic region, into the core of your body, up your spine and back, and into your chest. Take a deep breath and see the green and gold energy as touching and healing every cell and every organ.

See it moving into your shoulders, down your arms, into your elbows, forearms, wrist, hands, and fingers, green and gold energy healing every aspect of your being. Now again, go up your arms, into your shoulders, your back, up your neck, and into each sense organ—mouth, nose, ears, and eyes; and into your brain, bathing every aspect of your physical self with Divine Earth Mother's healing love and grace.

As the energy rises through your head, it spills over into your aura—the green and gold energy clearing and cleansing your aura. Focus on the top of your head, imagining a strong cord that connects you with your High Self and Higher Power. You are showered from above by the white light of Spirit creating an egg-shaped light surrounding and protecting you, reaching below your toes, stretching out past your fingertips, and to the top of your head.

Take a few moments to come back into the present. You might want to write in your journal about any experiences you had.

How do you feel at this moment? I like to ask my clients this question after doing the meditation together, as they usually appear surrounded by light and, sometimes, sparkles. Usually, they tell me they feel better emotionally and spiritually and are more present in mind and body.

HOW TO USE THE PENDULUM

When you first learn to dowse with the pendulum and align with your subconscious and super-consciousness, it is surprising, even elating, as the pendulum first moves seemingly of its own accord.

Again, anyone can learn how to use a pendulum. It is a natural, God/ Goddess-given skill. It is important to suspend the belief that you can't. Instead, simply imagine that you can learn to do this easily. It's sometimes helpful to say a few affirmations, such as

> *Spirit is guiding and directing my pendulum use and dowsing.*
> *My mind is open and receptive.*
> *All blocks on all levels have been removed.*
> *I learn new skills easily and quickly.*
> *Pendulum dowsing is fun and amazing.*

Follow these simple directions. [You can also use this exercise with the Yes/No and Clearing Signal Chart (1).]

1. Center yourself and relax with the centering or grounding meditations described earlier.

2. Hold the chain between your thumb and first finger. Make sure the chain hangs down four or five inches. (In the beginning, the shorter chain is easier to use.) See Figure 3-1.

3. Let the pendulum hang perfectly still.

4. Now train the pendulum to move and give you a *yes* answer. Keep your fingers, hand, or wrist still, and mentally ask the pendulum to move in a forward/backward movement or in the north/south direction. This movement is your *yes* answer. Then mentally tell the pendulum to stop moving.

5. Practice mentally saying the word *yes* and naturally moving your pendulum forward and backward, just as your head naturally moves up and down and nods *yes*. Do this a number of times until you are comfortable knowing that your pendulum is saying *yes*.

6. Mentally tell your pendulum to move side to side or in the east/west direction, just as your head will move back and forth when you mean *no*. This is your *no* answer.

7. Then tell your pendulum to stop moving.

8. Practice asking questions with *yes* or *no* answers. Start with simple questions that you know the answer to while you are training your consciousness and hand to dowse.

9. Continue to allow the pendulum to move without your hand influencing the decision. You may want to practice for a few days by asking *yes* or *no* questions before exploring the charts. If you feel you are ready, jump in and use the charts immediately. See how comfortable you feel and move at your own pace.

10. Expect a response and be in a receptive state for answers. Dowsing is a bit of a sister to faith.

A TEST TO SEE IF YOU'LL BE ABLE TO DOWSE WITH A PENDULUM

Take a breath, relax, and see if you and your pendulum are simpatico. Hold your pendulum over the palm of your other hand. In a moment or two, it should (without your moving it) start to move either in a clockwise or counterclockwise manner. Now you know you will be able to divine and use the pendulum with the Intuitive Healing Charts.

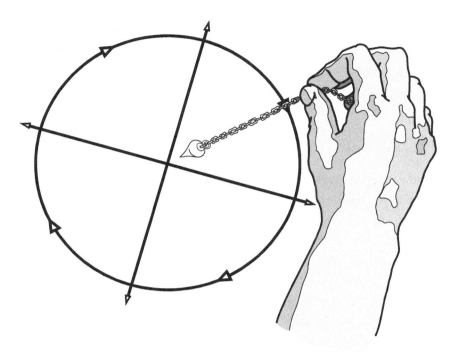

FIGURE 3-1

IF YOU ARE HAVING PROBLEMS

Imagine you are with me in a class. I am clearing everyone's psychic energy and helping everyone let go and dowse. I am here with you now. You have an inner child within—let go, let the child take charge, and see yourself easily learning the *yes* and *no* and clearing signals. You can do it.

We can be afraid we won't be able to actually perform—that dreaded performance anxiety! Yes, we all can have it. Or sometimes we can have blocks to dowsing that are either from a present or past life. Affirm the following sentences several times to clear your mind of skepticism:

Dowsing is Spirit's gift to me.
Dowsing is for my highest good and the good of others.
I completely erase all doubting thoughts now.
I easily and quickly learn to dowse.

Remember this is an exciting, enjoyable process. If you get frustrated, relax and try it at a later time. Try it early in the morning or evening when you have plenty of time and space. Much of this will begin to come naturally after practicing.

HOW TO CLEAR

Pendulum clearing is a one- or two-minute process to lighten and enliven our thinking and cleanse our energy. Because we lead busy lives, we can sometimes pick up negative, confused thoughts that can muddle our minds and cloud our auras. These can be either our own or other people's thoughts, ideas, and expectations. We often move too fast in life and can become scattered.

First, I'll teach you the clearing "signal." Hold your pendulum between your thumb and first finger. Ask your pendulum to move in a clockwise position. Your pendulum will begin to move in a clockwise motion. As it does so, ask the pendulum to clear your mind, thoughts, and energy. If you feel comfortable, take a few deep breaths and close your eyes. The pendulum will move and circle. (See Figure 3-2.) When your pendulum stops, you know you are cleared. You will feel a bit sharper and more awake. [You can also clear by using Yes/No and Clearing Signal Chart (1).]

A woman I was teaching to clear said, "We could all use this five times a day. It's so easy and yet powerful."

Clearing and Asking for Permission Before Beginning to Dowse

Ask:

- Am I clear?

- Am I working with my High Self? Are my answers 100 percent accurate?

If the answer is *no*, keep clearing until you are ready.

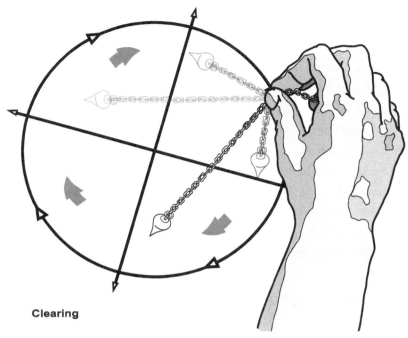

Clearing

FIGURE 3-2

The answer should be *yes* before you continue.

When doing a reading for another person, always ask:

- Do I have permission to work with this person?

- Is this for the highest good for this person?

If the answers are *no*, say a prayer for the person and see them surrounded by God/Goddess love and light.

The British Dowsers sum it up by asking:

- Can I? (Do I have the ability?)

- May I? (Do I have permission?)

- Should I? (Is it for the highest good of all?)

If you receive a *yes*, proceed.

INTUITIVE HEALING CHARTS

The next step is to learn to use the Intuitive Healing Charts with the pendulum. In the following four chapters, I'll introduce the charts with simple instructions and sample questions to ask. Take some time to turn to the end of the book and become familiar with the thirty-one Intuitive Healing Charts in the appendix. The first chart is a Table of Charts, which acts as a guide to the other thirty charts.

The Intuitive Healing Charts were developed to help you research your own healing challenges and solutions. At first, it might be a little overwhelming for you, but as you become more comfortable with using the pendulum in conjunction with the charts, you will see that they flow in a natural order. As you become more familiar, you will be able to do your research more quickly.

ASKING THE RIGHT QUESTIONS

It is so important to ask the questions carefully. In the beginning, it can be helpful to write down your questions so that you can see in black and white if your questions make sense and if these are truly the questions you want answered. The pendulum can be very precise. So if you're having problems getting a clear answer, review your question and rewrite it clearly.

BEGINNING TO DOWSE WITH THE YES/NO CLEARING CHART

Center and clear; see the earlier "How to Clear" section.

Start with the Yes/No and Clearing Signal Chart (1) in the appendix. Hold your pendulum over the center of the chart.

As you learned, the *yes* response is a forward-and-backward movement (north/south), and the *no* is a side-to-side movement (east/west). Ask questions that illicit a *yes* or *no* response.

Play and experiment. When you feel comfortable, begin experimenting with the charts.

RESEARCH—FINDING ANSWERS ON THE INTUITIVE CHARTS

After learning to dowse, you can turn your attention to the charts to help you formulate and receive answers. Each chart is a little different, so I've included instructions on each one in the next four chapters.

In Chapter 4, you will learn to use the Foundation Charts, which you will work with along with the other charts. In Chapter 5, you will explore the challenges that you have in this life using the Challenge Charts. In Chapter 6, you will realize you have solutions and many choices for healing. Often when ill, we feel the world closing in, when in truth there are many remedies. Remember you are unique. Use the Solutions Charts to find out what combination of treatments will work for you. Then in Chapter 7, you will face the ever-changing nature of life, transition, death, and rebirth.

(A reminder: Before beginning, center or ground yourself using the meditations described earlier, and center and ask permission as described in the "Clearing and Asking for Permission Before Beginning to Dowse" section.)

Start with the Yes/No and Clearing Signal Chart (1). You have already practiced without this chart, but now you can train the pendulum and mind to work with the charts. (As you learned previously, the perpendicular movement to and from the body is *yes*, just as if you were to nod *yes* with your head. The horizontal movement across the body is *no*, just as if you were shaking your head *no*.) As you practice, the subconscious, conscious, and super-conscious aspects of your mind are working with Spirit, searching for clues and receiving answers.

Now look at the Table of Charts (see page 163). This table leads to all the other charts. Place your pendulum over the middle of the black circle. You can practice by asking a general question, such as "What do I need to know today?" Your pendulum will begin to move toward an answer. Then you can proceed to the next chart your pendulum indicated.

Hang your pendulum over the black triangle or circle. Now hold it there as you ask a question of the chart. The pendulum will start moving in the direction of the answer.

To double-check your answer, you can put your pendulum over the word. If the answer is correct, it will start spinning. You can literally feel the energy of the word. Then you can ask a second question.

It is a good idea to methodically go through all the charts one by one, becoming familiar with them in order to practice using the pendulum with the charts. Remember that Chapters 4 through 7 include sample questions for each chart.

In Chapter 10, you will learn to give yourself a complete reading using all the charts.

Practice is key. Have fun while you learn this new and wonderful skill.

CONCERNS

Protection

I always begin a reading with a prayer calling on my spiritual guides. I work with the angels of light and love, the archangels, and Jesus and Mary. If, for any reason, I become afraid, then I call on them. Also, if you become afraid for any reason, call in Archangel Michael, as well as your guides, for protection, reassurance, and refuge. Put down the pendulum and charts, and wait until you feel safe again.

How Long Should You Dowse?

You have to be a little careful, especially in the beginning, not to overdo it. No more than two or three hours, to allow yourself to recharge.

If the Answers to Your Questions Don't Make Sense

Especially when you're new to dowsing, it's as if the pendulums have a mind of their own. Ask your question again and then

- Ask to be shown only one answer at a time. Ask for the most important answer on the chart to be revealed.

If the response seems totally off base, review these questions:

- Am I working with my High Self?

- Are my answers 100 percent accurate?

If the answer is *no*, keep clearing until you are ready.

Sometimes the answers won't seem to make sense. But write down the answers you receive anyway and see if they may make sense at a later time.

If you feel frustrated, take a break. Then come back to the process when you are more attuned.

APPRECIATE YOURSELF

By this time, after little or much practice, you may now have trained your mind and pendulum to give you *yes* and *no* answers and to clear. You likely have started experimenting with the pendulum and with the Intuitive Healing Charts.

As you start on this dowsing journey, you will learn to continue to trust yourself and the pendulum and the answers you receive. You are just beginning to move deeper into the thought-provoking aspects of working with your pendulum and the Intuitive Healing Charts.

CHAPTER 4

Foundation Charts

*You have the power to heal your life, and you need
to know that. We think so often that we are helpless,
but we're not. We always have the power of our
minds. . . . Claim and consciously use your power.*

—LOUISE L. HAY, *Meditations to Heal Your Life*

Now we turn to learning how to use the pendulum with the Intuitive Healing Charts, yet another source of fun and power in this book. After learning this simple but easy-to-use process that was once hidden but is now revealed to you, you will be amazed.

In the Foundation Charts, start with the Yes/No and Clearing Signal Chart (1), and review how to receive *yes* and *no* answers and clearing. Often, I have told students in my classes that if they learn nothing more than how to clear energy with a pendulum, they will have learned an important key to life.

With the Time and Percent Chart (2), you can discover in general terms the timing of future events and the likelihood of events happening. You can use it to dowse the positivity or negativity of a person, place, or thing. In the next chart, you examine a spiritual program to discover what could help you. In the Spiritual Guides Chart (4), you find just whom you are working with spiritually—sometimes it's surprising. Then you move on to your energy body and its layers, and the chakras and how to clear them. If you want to see what parts of your body might be affected physically, you can use the Physical Body Chart (7) and Body Systems Chart (8) to check out your physical organism and bodily systems.

It's best to review the Intuitive Healing Charts located in the appendix so that you are familiar with the chart information presented in this and subsequent chapters. Suggested questions are provided at the end of each chart section to use as examples until you are comfortable enough to formulate your own questions.

Just this is enough to keep a body and mind busy. This chapter is rich. Take your time to build a good foundation.

TABLE OF CHARTS

The Table of Charts (see page 163) is just like a table of contents. It lists all the charts in the Intuitive Pendulum Healing System and guides you to all the other charts where there are possible answers to your questions.

When looking for an answer, clarify the issue in your mind or on paper. You can do this by writing down a series of questions. In the beginning, it's a good idea to write down the questions, as you can verify on paper the questions and answers, and make sure the issue is clear to you. Then you can start at the Table of Charts.

To begin, hold your pendulum over the center oval of the Table of Charts. Ask, "What chart is needed?" Keep your eye on the pendulum, wait patiently, and let the pendulum guide you to the correct chart. In the beginning, it may take a few moments to move. If it swings wildly or goes to two or more answers, ask, "What chart is needed first?" Also, you can hold your pendulum over the word you think is correct. If it's right, your pendulum will feel the energy and spin clockwise.

Then go to the indicated chart, place the pendulum over the triangle or circle, and ask your question. After you are finished, return to the Table of Charts. Again ask, "What chart is needed?" Continue doing this until all of your questions are answered. When you return to the Table of Charts and the pendulum does not move, your healing is complete.

Remember: If more than one answer is given, ask, "Which chart should I go to first?"

Yes/No and Clearing Signal (Chart 1)

(See page 165.)

You and I are essentially infinite choice-makers.
In every moment of our existence, we are
in that field of all possibilities where we have
access to an infinity of choices.

—DEEPAK CHOPRA, *The Seven Spiritual Laws of Success*

By using the Yes/No and Clearing Signal Chart you are training the pendulum to give you correct signals. The perpendicular movement to and
from the body is *yes*, and horizontal movement across the body is *no*. As
you practice, your rational and subconscious mind is working with Spirit,
searching for answers.

This chart is for questions with *yes* or *no* answers and for clearing negative energy. When you're learning, it is helpful to use this chart until you
feel comfortable with the pendulum. When the pendulum moves forward and back, it means *yes*, and when it moves side to side, it means *no*.

You can practice using your pendulum to ask questions with *yes* or
no responses about anything you might want to know—from whether a
certain food is good for you to whether you should go on a trip. As soon
as you feel comfortable using the pendulum and receiving *yes* and *no*
answers, go to the other charts and practice as directed.

A little story—recently a student of mine had a spiritual reading with
me. We found that as a small child, she was unable to say *no* to her father
and keep her boundaries with him. When she tried practicing the Yes/
No and Clearing Signal Chart using the pendulum, the pendulum kept
saying, "*No, no, no.*" Another student at the next class pointed out that
it could have been her inner child learning to say *no*. That felt so right. I
cleared her, and she was able to dowse receiving both *yes* and *no* answers.
Clearing is important to a peaceful life. After you become more sensitive and intuitive, you'll be able to notice when your energy is clear and

when it isn't, and when physical spaces are and are not clear. By learning to clear with the pendulum, you'll be able to keep yourself, your home, car, and office cleansed of negative energy that can accumulate due to daily stress.

Clearing your mind of confusion and negative energy is a first step when using the charts. Also, when you are feeling fatigued or disturbed, try clearing yourself. You'll be amazed at how good this can feel and how it will shift your energy.

In Chapter 3, you learned that the clockwise motion indicates that the pendulum is clearing the energy. Practice this motion over this chart. Hold the pendulum at the center of the circle and say, "Please clear my mind, emotions, and spirit." Mentally tell the pendulum to move clockwise. This is your "clearing signal." Let the pendulum circle; when it stops, you are cleared. Also see the Clearing Needed Chart (16) to find out specifically what needs clearing. You will find that the more you clear your physical, mental, and spiritual self, the better you will feel.

Time and Percent (Chart 2)

(See page 167.)

We may want to know when an event is going to take place; certain decisions could be made more easily if we knew. Often, we cannot predict when someone is going to take an action in a given situation. You can use this chart to find out the general timing of an event. Know that the time can change because people change their minds.

For a serious decision, always give yourself permission to make it the following day. Take the time to mull over a situation, especially one that is emotional or has great impact. Rarely does anything need to be decided on the spot. It is better to make the right choice, even if it takes additional time, than the wrong decision in a hurried manner.

- What is the general time frame of this event, project, or situation?

Not only do we want to know when an event is going to take place, but we'd also like to know the likelihood of it taking place. With this chart you can ask, "How likely is it that this will take place?" Or it will help answer questions about your vitamins and medicines. You can ask, "How effective is this vitamin, cold medicine, or antibiotic?"

- What is the possibility this event or situation will happen?

Because we are constantly creating our own reality and others are creating theirs, predicting time and actions can be difficult. The universe is fluid, not fixed. Know that this is a general answer, rather than a final one.

Seek and Find Spirit (Chart 3)

(See page 169.)

In our materialistic society, many of us have ceased to believe in a personal God or a Higher Power. In life with all its ups and downs and all around, we may find ourselves seeking a deeper meaning. We may have the perfect job, home, and family, but we may feel something is missing. It might be the loss of a parent, loved one, or our own health that drives us to find Spirit. You might feel that your Higher Power has been attempting to get your attention for some years now. When we step on the spiritual path, we may be surprised at how comforting it can be to have a connection with Spirit.

Realize the Truth: In our lives we all have had that moment of truth when we know, just know, that what we have been telling ourselves is an illusion. As if we see with new eyes, we know we can no longer deny the truth.

Awaken: As you awaken through pain or joy, you will begin to notice how life feels a bit different, as if living in a new dimension. The life connections and intricate design of nature will become more evident and you will feel a new synchronicity in events. Ponder these questions: *What am I awakening to? Is it possible that a Higher Power exists? Could there be a divine plan for me?*

Ask for Help: This can be a simple prayer, "Help me." If you doubt, as most of us do, ask for help with a problem, large or small. Wait to see the answer appear in a synchronistic way. This is your Higher Power saying hello.

Spiritually Surrender: Ask that Spirit to come into your life and take charge of your ego, that selfish, demanding, critical part of the self whose motto is "me, me, me" that gets in the way. You can say a simple affirmation, such as "I surrender my life and ego to the care of Spirit." Let go and let God/Goddess. (P. S. Not to worry, you are giving up your little self to find your true Self.)

Clean Up the Past: First, write down your resentments, what happened, who was involved, and how the situation affected you. This can be a brief outline or more expanded if you want. Remember to include yourself on the inventory list, as you might have punished or hurt yourself in the past. Then share this list with someone you trust. Make a second list of every good quality you possess.

Ask Forgiveness: Forgiveness is a powerful tool that will free your soul. With your inventory in mind, first ask Spirit for forgiveness for the past of all people whom you may have harmed. Then forgive yourself. Then make amends to your family, friends, and others. Be sure to keep it on your side of the fence. No one needs to be blamed.

Let Go of the Past: So easy to say; so hard to do. I was haunted by my past until a minister said to me, "God has forgiven you. Who are you to not forgive yourself?" I would remind myself, "I am a child of God. Loved, forgiven, blessed!"

Practice Daily: Spend at least ten minutes in the morning and evening with Spirit. You can sit in silence, read inspirational books, or meditate on the good in your life. Some people do this before they get out of bed and others over a cup of coffee or tea. Remember to check in with your Higher Power, just as you would a friend. Then remember to give thanks at night before sleeping.

Be of Service: Ask your Higher Power how you can help others in your daily life. Is there a friend you could call? Could you help someone with errands, house repairs, or a ride? As you practice, you will be directed to those in need. What a blessing this can be. You will think less of yourself, your problems will grow smaller, and your mind will become quieter.

Be Mindful: As you wake and go through your day, instead of rushing out the door, rushing to work, and rushing through work, perhaps you could try the age-old practice of mindfulness. Simply pay attention to what you are doing as you are doing it—breathing, noticing, and practicing awareness of the moment.

- Where should I begin in the process?

- What do I need today?

- What else would be helpful?

Spiritual Guides (Chart 4)

(See page 171.)

The Spiritual Guides Chart is for those of us who want to know what spiritual help is available in any given situation. You can quickly find out. Just use this chart and ask. If you have another guide you would like to add to this chart, please feel free to do so.

Your guides are reminding you that you have much more support than you ever imagined. In fact, the angels and archangels in this day and age feel underutilized and appreciate it when we enlist their support.

You can ask your spiritual guides, angels, or deceased loved ones for help in every area of your life—material gifts, relationships, finances, or work. They cannot always change your fate, but they can ease the situation or journey. You can ask them for courage, strength, and perseverance to get through any situation.

The following is a brief description of the spiritual help available. I talk more about the angels because I am more familiar with them. Of course, many books have been written on these beings of the inner world. This is not a complete list. Please add your own spiritual helpers to your chart. Angels are light beings who help carry out God/Goddess's will and carry our prayers to heaven. The word *angel* means messenger, but they have many more duties and functions, including to care and comfort, protect, and guide us during our lifetime. When you hear an intuitive thought, it's most probably from your angel messenger.

Angels, for the most part, like being invisible to us. They appear when necessary, but they want us to be at ease, so at times they will assume human form as a mechanic, firefighter, or just a regular person that corresponds to our ideas of someone who naturally would assist us.

When we do have experiences with them, we feel their peaceful presence. When we are listening, we can hear their wise council. Angels are neither male nor female, though we often know them as either sex. With or without wings and sometimes in human form, they appear to help us.

Angels are not to be worshipped. Adulation is for God/Goddess alone. Communication with the angels is possible with practice and patience. If we are peaceful and centered, we can use the charts to feel and experience the angels.

I work with guardian angels and the angels of light and love, who help us in daily life with specific projects, and the archangels, who oversee larger life arenas.

Guardian Angels

Whatever our religious or spiritual beliefs, each of us has a guardian angel that we met before we came to earth. These guardian angels have been with us since birth and will be with us throughout our time as human beings on earth, and they will take our soul home when our body dies. We must remember we are never alone. The angels are commanding, yet they do not interfere with our lives or with our free will.

The Angels of Light and Love

The angels of light and love help us with any issue or challenge we might have in life. We can call on them to help us with human matters such as money, bills, jobs, resources, creativity, love, and relationships. They want to make life easier for us. When you ask your angels for help, you will find your life will be more fluid and synchronistic.

Archangels

The archangels are responsible for higher levels of human life. When I connect with them, I feel deeply honored to be with them. When I picture them in my mind's eye, I see immense, radiant beings. You too can feel their commanding energy and immeasurable love. The archangels and their legions of assistant angels that I am most familiar with and whom I have worked with most often are Michael, Gabriel, Uriel, and Raphael.

Michael is known as the "warrior of heaven" who leads God's armies. He is a protector—especially of women, children, police officers, and firefighters. Call on Michael and his assistants to protect and defend you in any situation.

Gabriel, the great messenger seen blowing a trumpet, is most famous for telling Mother Mary of the forthcoming birth of Jesus. Gabriel inspires us with God's thoughts and helps rouse humankind to action. Call on Gabriel and his assistants to communicate important, inspiring messages or speeches. Just remember to ask.

Uriel brings the gift of God's wisdom. I've seen him in yellow and white light, pouring out God's truth to humankind. If you are bewildered or perplexed as to whether something is true or not, ask Uriel for help. He will speak directly to your mind and heart.

Raphael, the archangel of healing and medicine, can be called upon for help in any emergency or with any medical problem. Say a short prayer, "Help!" and he will be there with you. I have experienced his energy as powerful green and gold shimmering light. Meditate with him and you will feel his healing power of light and love.

In Native American spirituality as well as other traditions, animal totems or power animals accompany us along our journey in life. They bring wisdom, knowledge, and power to the individual or group. The wise and encyclopedic book *Animal Speak* by Ted Andrews can guide you in finding and knowing your animal totems.

Enlightened beings who are no longer in the body and help human beings on earth are called ascended masters.

Gautama was an ascetic sage of the middle way (between the extremes of nihilism and nirvana) from whose teachings Buddhism was founded. He was recognized as a spiritual teacher who attained full enlightenment and shared his insights to help sentient beings to end rebirth and suffering.

A counselor can be a minister, therapist, or teacher who helps you on your spiritual path.

When we leave our physical bodies, we return to our true home in our spiritual form. *Deceased* refers to the physical body, not the spiritual one. When we dowse, we can contact our loved ones on the other side.

We all have an ego. When using the charts, it's necessary to work with our High Self. I placed "ego" on the chart, just in case we are making decisions with our lower consciousness.

Fairies are tasked to take care of all things in nature. Related to the angelic kingdom, they can be small to large in size, and powerful too.

I was first introduced to the fairy kingdom when I read about the Findhorn Community in Scotland, where Eileen and Peter Caddy and Dorothy Maclean communicated and were guided by the Devas and nature spirits. Once a sandy, barren land, today Findhorn is a thriving eco-village, a teaching center where residents and visitors are engaged in studying nature and spirit.

There are so many names for God—our Supreme Being. In Unity Church, God is viewed as neither male nor female, but as a spiritual energy, which permeates everything and is available to all people. Charles Fillmore, cofounder of Unity said, "God is not a person who has set creation in motion and gone away and left it to run down like a clock. God is Spirit, infinite Mind, the immanent force and intelligence everywhere manifest in nature. God is the silent voice that speaks into visibility all the life there is."[12]

By definition, a Goddess is a female deity. There are at least forty religions that have female deities, including the Egyptian, Grecian, Roman, and Wiccan.

Great Spirit is an English translation of the Sioux and other Native American names for the Supreme Being that created and rules over the universe.

You may find yourself being counseled from the other side. When I was painting daily, I felt and heard teachers from the invisible world.

Created as a broad encompassing term, *Higher Power* (HP) is used in twelve-step programs to refer to a Supreme Being or some conception of God. In Alcoholics Anonymous, people choose to define their own Higher Power.

That aspect of the self that is spiritual and is connected both to our bodies, but also to the spiritual world, is the High Self.

In Christian theology, the Holy Spirit is the third person in the Holy Trinity. Jesus himself was baptized with the "Holy Spirit." In *A Course in Miracles*, the Holy Spirit "calls to you, to let forgiveness rest upon your dreams, and be restored to sanity and peace of mind."[13]

Jesus is a historical figure who was a teacher and healer and whose life is reported in the Gospels of the Bible. He performed miracles throughout his ministry—healing people of disabilities, blindness, leprosy, and

[12] Charles Fillmore, *Talks on Truth* (Lee Summit, MO: Unity Books, 1912, 2007), 3–4.

[13] *A Course in Miracles*, "What Is the Holy Spirit?," *a.courseinmiracles.com/workbook-lessons /221-thru-290/what-is-the-holy-spirit.php#gsc.tab=0*.

mental illness. According to Helen Schucman, Jesus was the true author of *A Course in Miracles*. For further clarification, see "Clarification of Terms" in *A Course in Miracles*.[14]

A female disciple of Jesus who shared his ministry, Mary Magdalene was maligned and denigrated through the Middle Ages by the Catholic Church. It is important to note that in the Gospel of Mary, Levi defends her against Peter saying, "But if the Savior made her worthy, who are you indeed to reject her? Surely the Savior knows her very well. That is why He loved her more than us. Rather let us be ashamed and put on the perfect Man, and separate as He commanded us and preach the gospel, not laying down any other rule or other law beyond what the Savior said."[15]

Revered around the world, Mary can offer us love and compassion when we are most sad or bereaved. A saint in the Catholic Church, historically, she was a Jewish woman, the mother of Jesus.

Muhammad is the prophet and founder of Islam. Born in 573 in Mecca, he became an orphan in his childhood. His early years were spent in prayer in a cave, where he was visited by the angel Gabriel. Before his death, he united Arabia. His words and revelations are found in the *Quran*.

I like to call God "Spirit" because this name denotes an all-pervading, omniscient, and omnipresent God/Goddess.

Please add any other name to the chart that you are connected with so that you can use and check this chart!

- Who is helping me in this situation?

- Whose help do I need?

- Who can I call on when I need help?

- Who can I ask to help my friend, sister, brother, etc.?

---

[14] *A Course in Miracles*, "Clarification of Terms," *acourseinmiraclesnow.com/course-miracles-clarification-terms-jesus-christ/*.

[15] The Gnostic Society Library, "Gnostic Scriptures and Fragments, The Gospel According to Mary Magdalene," Chapter 9, verses 8 and 9, *gnosis.org/library/marygosp.htm*.

Energy Body—Auric Layers (Chart 5)

(See page 173.)

It has always been fascinating to me to know that we have an energy body—the aura, an electromagnetic energy field, which penetrates and surrounds us. In my first psychic healing class, we were taught to actually feel our auras, which of course made me a believer. Over the years, when I did healings and worked with a pendulum, I was able to see people's auras and chakras with my eyes closed.

Each auric layer has its own purpose and is connected to a specific chakra as follows:

- **Etheric:** connected with the first (root) chakra, is a life force battery, associated with or related to our organs, glands, nervous system, and chakra system; a glowing white oval shell.

- **Emotional:** connected with the second (sacral) chakra, changes the most in color, and is related to our feelings.

- **Mental:** connected with the third (solar plexus) chakra, is the place where our thoughts and ideas originate.

- **Astral:** connected with the fourth (heart) chakra, is a connective bridge to deliver love from higher levels to the first three chakras.

- **Etheric Body Template:** connected with the fifth (throat) chakra, contains a full imprint of the physical body.

- **Celestial Body:** connected with the sixth (third eye) chakra, is light, ethereal, and connected to the other side where we can see angels, guides, and spirits.

- **Ketheric Body:** connected with the seventh (crown) chakra; the energy emitted creates a gold and silver light and connects us to the spiritual planes that we return to at death.

Some of this information is from Kala Ambrose's book, *The Awakened Aura*, an excellent resource.[16]

You can use the pendulum to find out what aura levels are affected and what needs to be cleared and healed. Then say a simple prayer asking for clearing and use your pendulum to clear the layer.

- What layer needs clearing?

- What layer do I need to focus on for healing?

- What other layer needs attention?

Chakras (Chart 6)

(See page 175.)

Chakras are vital energy vortexes, or "spinning wheels," that connect the spiritual with the physical body. Aligned with a subtle energy channel and the spine, they start from the base of the spine and continue to the crown of the head. These chakras correspond to massive nerve centers in the body. They serve to accumulate, assimilate, and transmit psychological, physical, and spiritual energies and information. The chakras carry the life force, or prana, to various places in the body. Many spiritual healers can see, feel, and heal the chakras.

When a chakra is out of balance, it can affect the mental, emotional, and physical, as well as spiritual well-being of a person. In balance, a person can reach their full potential, realize higher states of consciousness, and become a cocreator with the God/Goddess.

[16] Kala Ambrose, *The Awakened Aura* (Woodbury, MN: Llewellyn Publications, 2011).

A great discussion of blocks to the chakras and health is C. Norman Shealy's book, *Medical Intuition*. Shealy, a neurosurgeon, psychologist, and founder of the American Holistic Medical Association, has seen thousands of patients over the years. He correlates much disease with untreated emotional issues related to the chakras.

The seven primary chakras, the location along the vertical axis of the body, and primary issues are

- The first, or root, chakra at the base of the tailbone is about safety— being grounded and connected to family and friends. When you are ungrounded, it's easy to forget, make mistakes, or physically injure yourself, as your energy isn't fully in the body. When I've had a psychological shock of some sort, I tend to energetically leap out of my body.

- The second, or sacral, chakra in the lower abdomen is related to sexuality, creativity, and financial security. When I was a single mom, I had many physical issues in this area and eventually had to have a hysterectomy. A wonderful psychic told me that if I wasn't working full time, running a business, and taking care of two teenagers, then I could most probably heal my uterus through visualization and diet. But because of my lifestyle, she strongly suggested I have the operation. I had already been to two doctors but had a difficult time trusting the traditional medical field. After my surgery, I was grateful for the psychic who was able to help me see the big picture and offered such great advice.

- The third or solar chakra is found in the solar plexus and is related to self-esteem, either too much or too little. Often when we have low self-esteem, we have weight issues. I too have suffered from low self-esteem and been a bit overweight all my life. Most probably this was related to all the spankings I received from birth to when I turned thirteen—at which point I told my father that if he touched me again, I would leave home.

- The fourth, or heart chakra is found in the chest at the heart and lung level and surrounding areas, and is about giving or receiving love. Dr. C. Norman Shealy's theory is that breast cancer is related to not receiving enough emotional nurturing. He posits that heart disease is caused by lifelong anger. Cancer is generally related to depression or the misperception of a person desiring that someone else, who is incapable of giving love, give the love and affirmation they so strongly want.

- The fifth, or throat, chakra is related to the ears, eyes, nose, throat, arms, and hands, and is the center of the will. When your will is too weak, you can't express needs or desires. If your will is too strong, you may be attempting to bend another's will to your own.

- The sixth, or third eye, chakra, located at the center of the forehead above the eyebrows, is related to disorders of the brain with unexpressed fear and negativity. A person may have been consciously or unconsciously lying to themselves in this or past lives.

- The seventh, or crown, chakra is located at the top of the head and is related to connectedness to God/Goddess and soul issues of meaning and purpose. Often we might ask, "Why me?" or be angry at God/Goddess for the circumstances of our life. We might not realize that we are to align our will with God/Goddess.

You can use this chart to discover if any of your chakras need clearing. I use it on myself, especially when I am having physical symptoms. Often, just by keeping the chakras clear, we can remain in excellent health. When we have a physical problem, we can check which chakras are affected and clear them. For example, if we have a cold, there is a possibility we've internalized sadness in our heart chakra. If we have been withholding information, we can block our throat chakra.

I've added hands and feet in the Chakras Chart because they are also extremely important and need to be cleared. Other smaller chakras exist too. Kala Ambrose, author of *The Awakened Aura*, believes they are connected to the acupuncture points, which she says are mini-chakras.

To clear the chakras, simply ask which chakra needs clearing. You can then go to the Limiting Thoughts Chart (14) and Feelings Chart (17) and ask what stuck energy, thought, or emotion needs to be cleared. After practicing this exercise over time, you might start to clairvoyantly see little pictures or mini-movies from a present or a past life. These are the blocks that you are clearing. Then you can just ask that the energy be cleared and subsequently be filled with the love and light of the angels. *You will see your pendulum spin until it's cleared. When it stops, the clearing is complete.*

You can further your studies of the chakras with Caroline Myss's book, *Anatomy of the Spirit.* Myss is a gifted medical intuitive who works with Dr. C. Norman Shealy and has studied the chakras firsthand—relating them to the body, soul, and spirit.

C. Norman Shealy and Caroline Myss together helped establish Holos University, which offers classes in and certifies Medical and Counseling Intuitives. See *www.holosuniversity.org* for further information.

A list of common ailments associated with the chakras can be found at *mychakras.wordpress.com/chakra-illness-directory/*.

For a chakra meditation, see Chapter 9.

- What chakra needs clearing or healing?

- What chakra needs strengthening?

- What other chakra needs assistance?

ANGELIC SUPPORT AND HEALING

All healing, no matter in what form, is what you might label self-healing.

—STEVAN THAYER AND LINDA SUE
NATHANSON, PhD, *Interview with an Angel*

When I have gone through difficult times, I have always called on the angels—especially when loved ones were sick. When my husband was ill, I got very close to the angels. I asked them to hold me and put me to sleep every night. I felt if I could sleep, I could take care of him the next day. I asked them to be in the car with me as I drove from Boulder Creek to San Francisco to take my husband for the next treatment or surgery. I asked them to help me with my business that I needed to keep running so that we could afford health insurance and have money for our living expenses.

The friend, caregiver, often the spouse, the one who ultimately is in charge of taking care of the sick person, also must remember to take care of themselves. They need healing too. They need extra self-care. Otherwise, how will they take care of their loved one?

I remember waking up six weeks after my husband had died, terrified because I was a single mom. I knew I would have many challenges—raising my preteens, running a company, and taking care of myself. I called on the angels one more time. Somehow I was filled with strength and courage, and they helped me sleep at night.

Today I use the Intuitive Healing Charts. I begin by asking questions with the Table of Charts: What do I need? What would be helpful? What type of healing would be effective? Is there someone I should go to? Is there something I need to look at in my life? What could be causing this? What is the root cause of this?

And when I have little aches and pains and fears about what's going on with my body, I ask the angels to help me. It's best to do this in the moments before bed. A simple request—"Please heal me"—is sufficient.

I cannot stress how comforting the angels can be during the most difficult times—such an unused resource and so available at a moment's notice. The angels want to interact, support, and love us! That is why they were created by God/ Goddess—to be our support team. Dr. H. C. Moolenburgh, a Dutch medical doctor and author of A Handbook of Angels, *says, "You do not really think we could do all this without some help, here at the bottom of the well of time."[17]*

Don't forget that we have many alternatives. Find what works best for you.

Physical Body (Chart 7)

(See page 177.)

The Physical Body Chart is included so you will have a reference chart to locate where an issue originates in your body.

It is important to remember how remarkable our bodies are and how every body is different. We all have lived in varied environments and have unique genetics.

Our bodies are attempting to communicate with us! It's obvious when we are hungry, tired, cold, or warm. Most of us respond by eating, sleeping, putting on a blanket, or taking one off.

But what of the more serious communications such as stress or pain? Often, we forget to just ask and then listen to our bodies.

We are taught to distrust our expertise or knowledge of our bodies, and to go to doctors for all our problems—to be fixed, be given a pill, or have surgery. But learning to trust your body and yourself is a process. Take the time to love and honor your body. Communicate with the body. Thank it, praise it, and love it. Treat it well by giving it clean water, great food, and exercise. Let go of anything that is hurting your body.

---

[17] H. C. Moolenburgh, *A Handbook of Angels* (Essex, England: C. W. Daniel Company Limited, 1988), 64.

When you notice a small ache or pain, you can ask your angels to remove it and ask for healing.

Here are some suggestions for you to improve your relationship with your body:

- Treat your body with love and respect.

- Remember, your body is self-healing.

- Give your body enough rest.

- Fuel it with a variety of healthy, wonderful foods.

- Exercise and enjoy your body.

- Have fun in life.

Resist the pressure to judge yourself and others based on weight, shape, or size. Respect people based on the qualities of their character and accomplishments, rather than on their appearance. Remember to listen to your body. And don't forget to thank your body for all it does for you twenty-four hours a day.

- What part of my body needs healing?

- What other part of me needs healing? (Mental, emotional, or spiritual?)

- What other part of me is physically being affected?

- What do I need/desire for my total healing?

Body Systems (Chart 8)

(See page 179.)

We have amazing inner systems that work together to keep us healthy. Explore and discover more about the various body systems by going to *www.innerbody.com* for detailed information and interactive diagrams.

Now here's a basic list of the body systems:

- **Cardiovascular:** Includes the blood, vessels, and heart, which circulates the blood, delivers oxygen and nutrients to cells and organs, and removes waste.

- **Digestive:** Includes the mouth, esophagus, stomach, and intestines to digest food and remove waste.

- **Endocrine:** Includes glands and hormones that provide a communication system within the body.

- **Immune:** Includes the lymph, tonsils, spleen, bone marrow, white blood cells, and antigens that provide protection and repairs the body.

- **Integumentary (skin):** Includes skin, hair, nails, and glands that cover the body and regulate the temperature.

- **Lymphatic:** Includes lymph nodes, vessels, lymph, and other lymphoid organs that balance and defend against pathogens.

- **Muscular:** Includes muscles that attach to the bone for movement and posture.

- **Nervous:** Includes the brain, spinal cord, and nerves for processing sensory information and regulating the body.

- **Renal/Urinary:** Includes the kidneys, ureter, bladder, and urethra for filtering and excreting urine.

- **Reproductive:** Includes the sex organs of men and women for producing children.

- **Respiratory:** Includes the nose, lungs, and trachea to conduct air to and from the body.

- **Skeletal Articular:** Includes bones, joints, and cartilage that provide structure and support for the body.

- What body system is under stress?

- What body system could use help?

- What body system needs strengthening?

Type of Healing Needed (Chart 9)

(See page 181.)

I added this chart because I knew it might be important to know what type of healing is necessary—emotional, mental, physical, or spiritual. For most of us, we might notice that something is wrong with our energy or body—a sensation or a feeling, or an ache or a pain. We might have an intuition or a dream about the fact that healing is needed. Usually, we'll need healing of both thoughts and emotions.

Recently, I began seeing flashing lights in front of my eyes. I made an appointment to see my doctor and then was referred to an ophthalmologist. When I checked this chart, the response prompted me in the direction of both emotional and physical healing.

I immediately took action. I remembered to ask the angels for a healing and to be guided to the right and perfect healers to help me. I wrote in my journal and asked, "What was I not wanting to see?" Then at my poetry class later that day, I wrote a poem expressing the sad and troubling world events of late. I realized I was attempting not to see them. I also wrote an affirmation, "I see with the eyes of Christ." Whenever I became anxious about my eyes, I said a prayer, and said my affirmation.

Use this chart to find out what type of healing is needed. Then ask for spiritual guidance. Sometimes we are surprised by the answers.

- Where is the healing that is needed first?

- Where else is the healing needed?

TYPES OF PROBLEMS THAT REQUIRE WESTERN MEDICINE

At times what the body needs is Western medicine. Seek immediate medical help if you are experiencing a serious problem such as

- *Acute infections*

- *Acute significant pain*

- *Burns*

- *Changes in consciousness*

- *Chest pain*

- *Difficulty breathing—shortness of breath*

- *Drug emergency*

- *Heavy bleeding*

- *Lump in chest or body*

- *Major trauma*

- *Paralysis or loss of sensation*

- *Poisoning*

- *Prolonged high fever*

- *Severe allergic reaction*

- *Severe headache*

- *Severe injury (such as an accident)*

- *Shock*

- *Signs of a heart attack or stroke*

- *Sudden, severe pain*

- *Vision problems or loss of vision*

If you are wondering whether you should go to a doctor or emergency room—go. It's much better (the adage) to be safe than sorry!

CHAPTER 5

The Arduous Path—The Challenge Charts

*It is among the most basic human truths: Every one
of us, some day, will be brought to our knees—by
a diagnosis we didn't expect, a phone call we can't
imagine, or a loss we cannot endure.*

—CONGRESSMAN JOE KENNEDY III,
Speech in the House of Representatives, March 8, 2017

I like the idea of staying healthy, eating well, exercising, sleeping just the right amount, and attempting not to get too stressed out about life. I just don't like being sick. Nobody does. But we are all spiritual beings living in a human body, and sometimes our minds, bodies, and spirits need extra care to come into balance. Other times there is an unexpected, full-blown emergency.

Facing any illness can be the hardest of life's challenges.

This chapter includes six charts that help us understand the cause of illness we may be facing, our life stressors, possible addictions, the type of healing needed, blocks to healing, and limited thoughts that may be contributing to our disease.

I always want to know why. I'm just curious. These charts attempt to answer these questions:

- Why do I have this issue?

- What are the causal issues?

I also want to know if my problem is spiritual, physical, mental, or emotional. The reason is that you may take a long look at the difficult issue you may be facing and figure out how you can approach your healing.

The power of this chapter resides in the fact that if we can face the true cause of our challenge, then we have the ability, with Spirit's help, to transform ourselves and heal. While we are living through this process, it's important not to blame ourselves but to love and give ourselves credit for awakening, releasing, and becoming new.

Factors Contributing to Disease (Chart 10)

(See page 183.)

First, let me say I am not a trained medical professional; I am an intuitive dowser. I was curious to know what the overall causative factors of illness were. This is a considerable topic that is still being researched and studied today. Dr. C. Norman Shealy's books *Medical Intuition* and *Energy Medicine* employ a holistic view of the causes of disease, separating them into two main categories—those with *psychospiritual roots* and those with *physiological roots*.

The body always attempts to communicate. Our aches and pains can tell us what we have been thinking. For example, when you notice you have a crick in your neck, you might have been saying to yourself, "They are a pain in the neck." But remember, you are the one who receives the neck pain. You may need to examine your relationships with others. Or another example—if you can't stand something and you get a stomach-ache, you might be telling yourself, "I can't stomach that."

Whenever I start to get a sore throat, I ask myself first, "What am I withholding? Who don't I want to tell the truth to?" It's a sign to me I need to be honest with my feelings and perhaps communicate with others. If you listen to the pain in your body and what you have been saying, you will notice the connection. Then you can correct your thinking and heal.

Often we can experience inner stress caused by conflict between our differing selves. For instance, our human self may want to acquire material goods, while our spirit self may have a soul plan for us. In our overly busy and often frantic world, we may forget our earthly mission. We may not be in touch with our soul. Through the body, the soul may be attempting to get our attention. And the soul will persist until, hopefully, we listen. I've gotten better at listening because I don't like pain or suffering, or even the common cold.

Through our bodies, our soul is giving us a strong message and we are forced to listen.

- What is your body attempting to tell you?

- What is the metaphor of the illness?

Sometimes we may have veered from our soul path. We can write a list of our aims in life, and then we may discover our purpose. We can ask the questions:

- Is my life on course?

- According to my soul, am I in the right work?

- Am I doing all that I am supposed to be doing on earth?

- Is there something else I should be doing?

- What is my soul's purpose?

Louise L. Hay was a prolific writer and publisher on the body-mind-spirit connection. In her book *You Can Heal Your Life*, she tells how she changed her thoughts and healed from cancer. Hay has created a chart of the primary illnesses with the messages they might be sending and an affirmation to correct your thinking. Whenever I have an issue, I check her book, and usually the information is correct.

Another favorite book on the subject is Deepak Chopra's *Reinventing the Body, Resurrecting the Soul,* which offers a breakthrough perspective on how the body and soul can flourish together.

In another book, *Energy Healing,* Dr. Shealy lists the psycho-spiritual roots related to disease—fear of death, fear of being invalid, poverty, abandonment, loss of love, and fear of existence—which he believes lead to all harmful mental/emotional reactions such as anxiety, guilt, anger, and depression.

I certainly have experienced all of these fears at one time or another, and I too have felt these reactions. As soon as I understand my thoughts and emotions, I process them by writing, talking with a friend or counselor, and then releasing them.

The U.S. Centers for Disease Control and Prevention (CDC) estimates that eliminating three risk factors—poor diet, inactivity, and smoking—would prevent 80 percent of heart disease and stroke, 80 percent of Type 2 diabetes, and 40 percent of cancers.[18]

When we do not have clean air and water and when we eat poorly, we cannot expect to be healthy. Most chronic diseases are caused by pollution, bad eating habits, addictions, and lack of exercise. We need to up our game!

If we are deficient in any of our basic human requirements for life, we may become ill. These privations may include lack of fresh air, clean water, healthy food, nutrients, sunlight, exercise, love, purpose, or rest.

Here are some other causative factors:

- **Accidents:** They can be caused by lack of attention but are sometimes unavoidable.

---

[18] National Center for Chronic Disease Prevention, *The Power of Prevention: Chronic Disease... the Public Health Challenge of the 21st Century,* 2009, https://www.cdc.gov/chronicdisease/pdf/2009-Power-of-Prevention.pdf.

- **Addictions:** Such addictions, especially to sugar, cigarettes, and alcohol, contribute to disease. See the Addictions Chart (12) for specific addictions.

- **Emotional Stress:** Stress robs the body of vital energy, suppresses immune function, and disrupts hormonal systems. The cumulative result can be devastating. Check the Life Stressors Chart (11) for different types of stress.

- **Erroneous Beliefs:** Deep seated, often formed as an infant or child, and subconscious, these beliefs may no longer serve us and can block and prevent us from healing.

- **Genetic Predisposition:** Genetic predisposition means we are born with a specific condition or with a genetic susceptibility.

- **Immune Deficiencies:** Deficiencies occur when our immune systems are either weak or overly active.

- **Infections:** Infections are caused by microbes such as bacteria, fungus, viruses, or parasites. Some are not so serious, such as the common cold, and others, such as AIDS, are potentially life threatening.

- **Inflammation:** Inflammation is caused by free radicals that are continually generated as a by-product of energy production. It is the root of inflammation in the body.

- **Internal Conflict:** Such conflict can be caused by stress between our body, mind, emotions, and soul.

- **Lack of Exercise:** An inactive lifestyle can make the body stagnant and the mind slow, and is a major cause of chronic conditions.

- **Lack of Healthy Food:** Though we may live in the land of plenty, our supermarket shelves are filled with tempting "junk" food. Avoid those aisles, and head for the fresh fruits, vegetables, and health food section.

- **Lack of Sleep:** Many of us today are sleep deprived from having too much fun on our electronic devices. But sleep deprivation over time can cause serious mental and physical health problems.

- **Lack of Sunlight:** We need our daily short dose of sunlight to keep us mentally and physically healthy. A lack of sunlight can be serious for those affected by depression and Seasonal Affective Disorder (SAD).

- **Loneliness:** This feeling tells us we need to find new friends and connect with them. Sometimes we spend too little time truly communicating and being authentic with others. Consider joining a group, church, or class to find new friends.

- **Mental, Emotional, or Physical Imbalance:** Such imbalances occur when we are conflicted, too busy, too stressed, and tired.

- **Negative Thoughts:** A common problem within many people's minds is having negative thoughts. Read the classic *The Power of Positive Thinking,* by Norman Vincent Peale.

- **No Purpose:** Without purpose, we flounder. To find purpose, ask in meditation and prayer what Spirit's will is for you. It might become clear in a conversation with a friend or even a dream. If you keep asking, you will hear and know your purpose.

- **Nutritional Deficiency:** When the body doesn't absorb or get enough of the right vitamin, mineral, or food, it experiences a nutritional deficiency.

- **Past Life Issue:** Is something from a past life blocking your healing?

- **Present Life Issue:** Did something happen when you were a baby, child, or adolescent? Take the time and energy to discover and clear these issues.

- **Radiation:** Natural radiation is present in our environment, such as gamma rays, X-rays, and ultraviolet (UV) radiation from the earth, sun, and space. Unnatural radiation is manmade, such as that found in electronics, and has been steadily increasing.

- **Script:** A script is a subconscious story (based on false beliefs) that we are creating and following in this life that no longer serves us, but prevents us from being healthy no matter what we do.

- **Toxins:** Toxins are petroleum based and can be ingested through breathing or absorption through the skin, as well as from pesticides in our foods or gardens. It's important to limit these as much as possible.

- **Traumas:** Physical and emotional wounds that need medical and therapeutic care cause trauma.

- **Unaddressed Feelings:** Use the Feelings Chart (17) to find what emotions you need to uncover and clear.

- **Unclean Air:** Though we can't always control air quality, we can take measures to live in a healthy place.

- **Unclean Water:** Make sure the water you drink is filtered and clean.

Remember—if you have any severe symptoms, seek medical help immediately.

Life Stressors (Chart 11)

(See page 185.)

The Holy Spirit will help you reinterpret everything you perceive as fearful, and teach you that only what is loving is true.

—*A COURSE IN MIRACLES* (TEXT, page 74)

In *The Healing Code*, Alexander Loyd, PhD, ND, and Ben Johnson, MD, report, ". . . almost all health issues originate from one problem—stress."[19] When I checked other statistics, they varied. The U.S. Centers for Disease Control says stress is related to 90 percent of all disease. Dr. Andrew Weil, an American physician and author who is broadly described as a "guru" for holistic health, says that nearly half of all Americans suffer adverse effects from stress. Stress has been linked to the leading causes of death: heart disease, cancer, accidents, and suicide.

We've all experienced stress: pressure, strain, anxiety, tension, or trauma. There are two types of stress: acute (short term) and chronic (long term). Acute stress occurs when we have a sudden, dangerous, or life-threatening situation, and our body's fight-or-flight response is automatically activated. For example, on a two-lane highway, when we just miss a car that drifted over to our lane, our stress levels shoot sky high!

Our fight-or-flight system can be activated many times a day, as we respond to emotionally difficult situations all day long. For instance, we have a disagreement with our spouse; we are a few minutes late to work already and encounter heavy traffic that is going to make us even later; there are endless deadlines at work and not enough time.

Here are ten suggestions to minimize stress:

- Make a list of what might be causing stress in your life.

- Start keeping a record of stressful events.

- Create a journal of thoughts and emotions, which is helpful to knowing the Self.

---

[19] Alexander Loyd, with Ben Johnson, *The Healing Code* (New York, NY: Hachette Book Group, 2010), 42.

- Figure out ways in which to let go of stressful work, relationships, or situations.

- Create and strengthen your other positive friendships.

- Communicate more with family and friends.

- Learn how to express your thoughts and feelings.

- Learn the power of saying *no* when someone asks you to do something you don't want to truly do.

- Investigate your true purpose in life and move in that direction.

- Simplify your life and do more of what you truly love.

I highly recommend *The Healing Code*, which describes a process for identifying the cause of the stress and transforming deeply embedded beliefs. You can experiment and see whether the exercises work for you. Numerous clients and I have used it for physical, mental, and emotional release, and have been amazed at the results.

Use the Life Stressors Chart to discover the causes of your stress. Then use the other Intuitive Healing Charts to look for solutions.

- What is causing the stress in my life?

- What areas of my life do I need to address?

- What areas of my life could I simplify so I have less stress?

- How can I manage my life so there is less stress?

- What could I add to my life (exercise, healthy food, or better vitamins) to decrease the stress?

Addictions (Chart 12)

(See page 187.)

First of all we had to quit playing God.

—BILL WILSON, Cofounder of Alcoholics Anonymous

Addiction in the United States today is rampant. In some form or another, directly or indirectly, we are all impacted—perhaps by family, friends, or ourselves, who may be suffering from the effects of drug, alcohol, or tobacco addiction. The following statistics show how huge the problem has become:

Estimates of the total overall costs of substance abuse in the United States, including productivity and health- and crime-related costs, exceed $600 billion annually. This includes approximately $193 billion for illicit drugs, $193 billion for tobacco, and $235 billion for alcohol. As staggering as these numbers are, they do not fully describe the breadth of destructive public health and safety implications of drug abuse and addiction, such as family disintegration, loss of employment, failure in school, domestic violence, and child abuse.[20]

Alcoholics Anonymous (the original twelve-step program) views alcoholism as a spiritual problem that affects all levels of our being—physical, mental, and emotional. When people have worked the Twelve Steps, many have a spiritual awakening as described in the A.A. literature:

When a man or a woman has a spiritual awakening, the most important meaning of it is that he has now become able to do, feel, and believe that which he could not do before on his unaided strength and resources alone.

---

[20] National Council on Alcohol and Drug Dependence, "Facts about Alcohol," July 25, 2015, www.ncadd.org/about-addiction/alcohol/facts-about-alcohol.

He has been granted a gift, which amounts to a new state of consciousness and being.[21]

Alcoholism and addiction are devastating and life threatening. In the beginning, alcohol and drugs can seem like so much fun—a little alcohol as a teenager or a little experimentation with pot seems harmless enough. Approximately 10 percent of the U.S. population will become addicted to a life-threatening substance or addictive behavior sometime in their life. Presently, millions need help.

If you've ever been in the grips of alcoholism or drug addiction, you definitely feel out of control. No matter how many times you told yourself, "I'm just going to have one or two" or "I'm not going to drink or use today," you may find yourself breaking promises. In the latter stages, you may have simply accepted you need to drink that pint or quart. As they say in twelve-step programs, "We were powerless."

Addiction is a disease and the addicted person needs help. What is amazing to note is that help is available through twelve-step programs and it's free. It is no longer considered shameful to go through a program or rehabilitation. Many people, including celebrities and spiritual seekers, have shared their struggles and recovery, moving from hopelessness to hope.

If you are struggling with these issues, know that you do not have to fight your addiction alone. You can find a group of people who have gone through withdrawal, have learned to live comfortably without alcohol or drugs, and have rebuilt their lives.

So seek and ye shall find help.

Use the Addictions Chart to discover your primary and secondary addictions. Many of us can have multiple addictions. Do not get too overwhelmed. It's wise to work on one addiction at a time. Focus on the

---

[21] Alcoholics Anonymous, *Twelve Steps*, "Step Twelve," https://www.aa.org/pages/en_US/twelve-steps-and-twelve-traditions, (pdf) 106–7.

addiction that is harming you the most. Seek help either through a counselor or a twelve-step program.

- Do I have an addiction I need to look at?

- What is my primary addiction?

- What is my secondary addiction?

- What addiction is harming me?

- What addiction is stopping me from having a full life?

MIRACLES

In my twenties, I was on a destructive path into full-blown alcoholism. I will not give you the details, but believe me, I could have died a number of times before I finally found Alcoholics Anonymous at the age of thirty. I went to my first meeting in the summer of 1982. There were six women in that pine-paneled room, and one of the women became my A.A. sponsor. I followed directions, began working the Twelve Steps, and never drank again. One crazy, wonderful miracle!

Here are a few other miracles that happened in my first few months of sobriety.

I had to leave California after being sober for six weeks and return alone to finish my teaching contract in Sao Paulo, Brazil, a city of twelve million people. My new apartment was within walking distance of the American Church, where the only English-speaking meeting of A.A. was held once a week. I attended faithfully and stayed sober.

My girlfriend, who knew I had just joined A.A., sent me a book, Love Is Letting Go of Fear, by Gerald Jampolsky. When I looked at the package, I noticed there was no P.O. box number or ZIP code. Then I looked at the date stamp. That little miracle book arrived in Brazil within two weeks! In those days, it often took six weeks for a letter to arrive; and often letters and packages never arrived at all.

Jampolsky's book was my introduction to A Course in Miracles, *which had a profound influence on my mind and life.*

My girlfriend also sent me the Daily Word, *a little Unity publication. While my housemates drove, careening through the streets of Sao Paulo, I sat in the backseat of a little Volkswagen reading the* Daily Word, *which helped me stay balanced and find my spiritual connection to God. That was my introduction to the Unity Church, and its prayers and affirmations.*

Perhaps the biggest miracles came in the summer of 1982. First, my sister, Therese, arrived at A.A.'s door two weeks before me. Second, my mom, who was physically dying of alcoholism, got sober. My mom lived for five more years. Therese and I have stayed sober now for thirty-six years!

These events all led me to working in the prayer room at Unity Village and studying A Course in Miracles. *So yes, I believe in miracles. Miracles—all of us!*

Blocks to Healing (Chart 13)

(See page 189.)

As terrifying as disease is, it is also an invitation to enter into the nature of mystery.

—CAROLINE MYSS, *Why People Don't Heal and How They Can*

We may be harboring old ideas or beliefs that prevent us from healing. It's good to look at these. I have worked with some people who receive a benefit from having a disease. We think, who wouldn't want to heal? But perhaps they receive a monthly disability payment, and they're afraid of losing the financial support. Or other people may take care of them, and they love the attention; they're afraid that without their illness, they wouldn't get the same love, the same care.

Sometimes people are so identified with an illness that they have taken it on as an identity. Author Caroline Myss calls this "woundology." If you find this is true for you, take time to write in your journal about the issue; write what about the illness is positive and negative for you. If you decide you want to let go of this, then clear it. You may have to try clearing it more than once, as this can be a deep issue.

Sometimes, I have clients who need clearing of their past lives. Often in a past life there could have been a physical injury or death that still affects this present life. I find the information in a person's chakra, like a little movie. It can be somewhat strange, sitting in my beautiful, comfortable loft, to suddenly see in my mind's eye, the person sitting before me, going through death by torture or mutilation. Some people want more details, but others just want the past life cleared immediately. I say a prayer and use my pendulum.

Clearing a person of spiritual blocks and past life issues frees that person from the past and its issues and promotes spiritual growth. This has led to improved health in many of my clients.

- Am I consciously blocking my ability to heal?

- Am I *un*consciously blocking my ability to heal?

- Why am I blocking my ability to heal?

- What am I getting out of being sick?

- What part of me is not listening?

- Is it a past life, present life, or future life issue?

- What am I learning?

- What is the gift the illness is giving me?

- What spiritual insight am I receiving?

Limiting Thoughts (Chart 14)

(See page 191.)

Limiting thoughts may have been lodged in our minds for years and have their roots in our subconscious. It's so important to examine our thoughts and weed out the negative ones that may be causing us harm, both emotionally and physically. The shackles we created in the past may prevent us from healing in the present. There is a simple solution. It just takes time and persistence. Use this chart to research your limiting thoughts. Then with the Empowering Thoughts Chart (15), you will be able to change your thoughts and change your life.

It's also good to listen to your own thoughts, especially when you might be angry or upset at yourself. If you catch yourself in the act, saying something mean to yourself, you can change your thought. Who hasn't said to themselves after an accident, "I'm so clumsy" or "I'm so stupid." I like to use the quick form of denial and say, "Cancel, cancel," and "Oh, I just made a mistake. I forgive myself."

Our thoughts have an incredible impact on our lives, influencing us both positively and negatively. If you set up a goal or intention, it is important to identify what thoughts are behind it. Often we are being run—unconsciously—by old, unproductive thoughts we picked up as children, thoughts so ingrained we don't realize that we are repeatedly giving ourselves negative messages, such as "I am always going to be sick."

For example, what if your goal is to heal, and your subconscious believes you cannot recover? What will happen? Nothing. You cannot create healing from a place of limited thoughts or beliefs, only positive ones. I encourage you to use this chart to begin the process of converting your limited thoughts into positive ones. When this begins to occur, you will feel a corresponding lightness to your spirit.

As the Buddha said, "The mind is everything. What you think, you become."

- What belief is blocking my healing?

- What don't I want to look at?

- Am I being truthful?

- What thought could I let go of?

- What else is preventing my healing?

CHAPTER 6

Many Paths to Healing—The Solutions Charts

*No problem can be solved from the same level of
consciousness that created it.*

—ALBERT EINSTEIN

If we can rise above our issues and see them in a broader, higher way, we can work with ourselves to solve many of our health problems. When a traditional doctor tells you there is no cure, you know it's time to turn to alternative medicine and find what else could work for you. Never give up!

So much in healing has to do with belief. Studies on the placebo effect (defined as a favorable response to a medical intervention—a pill, a procedure, a counseling session that doesn't have a direct physiological consequence) shows it can work 30 to 50 percent of the time. The placebo effect points to the fact that when people think they are getting a treatment that will help them, they in fact do heal. It's a clear example of mind over matter. In "Putting the Placebo Effect to Work," we learn that when people receive caring attention, the placebo effect is even stronger.[22] Make sure your health professionals are empathetic and caring.

This chapter provides solutions to our healing challenges on all levels: spiritually, mentally, emotionally, and physically. The chapter begins with empowering thoughts.

....

[22] Harvard Health Letter, "Putting the Placebo Effect to Work," April 2012, *www.health .harvard.edu/mind-and-mood/putting-the-placebo-effect-to-work.*

As Edgar Cayce, the great medical intuitive, said, "Mind is the builder."

In the Clearing Needed Chart (16) included in this chapter, you can figure out what energetic cleansing is required, whether it be in your home, car, or body. The next four charts explore feelings and human needs and take us into the heart of healing; you will learn what self-care is needed and what healing arts would be helpful for you. You will investigate what vitamins and minerals your body might be lacking and what food is best for you. At the end of this solution-based chapter, I've also included charts on flower essences, aromatherapy, and crystals, which are safe, yet powerful, energetic remedies you can make and use for yourself.

Empowering Thoughts (Chart 15)

(See page 193.)

After clearing limiting thoughts, we can replace them with "empowering thoughts." Really, it's that simple. *Words are power. When you change your words and transform your thoughts, you can change your reality.* Yes, it takes time and repetition, but it's well worth the effort. On the Empowering Thoughts Chart, let your pendulum find the words you need so you can create new, positive affirmations for your life.

First, check the Limiting Thoughts Chart (14), and ask:

- What negative word(s) am I holding on to?

- What thought needs to be cleared?

Use your pendulum and say, "High Self, please clear my negative thought." You will see your pendulum moving in a clockwise motion. Next, go to the Empowering Thoughts Chart (15). Have your pendulum choose one or two powerful words, and practice the Powerful Words Meditation.

Sit in a comfortable chair and relax.

Breathe in and out, becoming aware of your chest rising and falling.

Imagine that in your mind/body there is a serene lake. Drop the powerful word(s) you have chosen from the Empowering Thoughts Chart (15).

Create a simple statement to repeat, starting with "I am." For example: "I am totally trusting the process of healing."

Inhale and silently repeat to yourself, "I am."

Exhale and silently repeat to yourself, "totally trusting the process while healing."

The words fall one by one into the consciousness of your being, becoming a part of you.

Repeat this cycle for three to five minutes.

Then use the affirmation you have created, and post it where you can see and repeat it several times daily.

- What words do I need to empower myself today?

- What words will help heal this situation?

- What words will help me heal?

THE POWER OF AFFIRMATIVE PRAYER

I was on a new spiritual path, living in Unity Village in Missouri, where I worked for Silent Unity in the prayer room seven hours a day, five days a week. In my off hours, I walked through Myrtle Fillmore's rose garden and apple orchard, and I wondered, How did I ever get here? Do I belong? Oh my gosh, I'm working in a prayer room!

Silent Unity trained me in affirmative prayer. Here is a description of affirmative prayer from the current Unity website: "Rather than begging or beseeching God, this method involves connecting with the spirit of God within and asserting positive beliefs about the desired outcome."[23] *Affirmative prayer is the same method of prayer Jesus taught when he said, "So I tell you, whatever you ask for in prayer, believe that you have received it, and it will be yours."*[24]

Sometimes people would call crying, saying, "I'm sick. I'm just diagnosed. I am so scared." Or "My mother just was diagnosed." Or "My husband, my father, my best friend." We learned to listen and say comforting words. Then we prayed earnestly with them and sent them a follow-up letter with a written affirmation. Powerful!

I received a small salary for praying with people from around the world. But the biggest reward was that praying with other people healed me, healed my mind. Even though I had worked the Twelve Steps in A.A., I still had many unkind thoughts about myself. Intellectually, I knew I was forgiven, but I hadn't forgiven myself in my mind and heart. In the prayer room, a part of me was beginning to heal. I heard a new voice in my mind that said, This is who you really are. This is your true self. You are loved. You are a child of God. You can help yourself and others.

While living there, I felt close to Myrtle Fillmore. I read her books. I communed with her as I walked and prayed. Here are her own words from her papers and her healing journey:

> The light of God revealed to us—the thought came to me first—that life was of God, that we were inseparably one with the Source, and that we inherited from the divine and perfect Father. What that revelation did to me at first was not apparent to the senses. But it held my mind above negation, and I began to claim my birthright and to act as though I believed myself the child of God, filled with His life.[25]

....

[23] See *www.unity.org/prayer/what-affirmative-prayer.*

[24] Mark 11:24 (NIV).

[25] Unity, "In the Words of Myrtle Fillmore," *www.unity.org/resources/articles/words-myrtle-fillmore.*

I lived in Unity Village for nine precious months. Amazing! What a miracle. Remember, prayer is such a powerful method for healing and it can be used anywhere and every day of our lives.

Clearing Needed (Chart 16)

(See page 195.)

Clearing is a powerful dowsing technique. Once you learn how to clear, you will find yourself clearing every aspect of your life—from your bedroom to your kitchen, from your aura to your chakras.

Clearing is just what it sounds like—an energy bath using the pendulum. It's a method to change and shift energy. You can use it to transform your own energy, or the energy of your house, car, or office. After dowsing for a while, you will be able to know when you are clear, and feel the difference between cleared and uncleared spaces.

Practice the clearing technique as given in the Yes/No and Clearing Signal Chart (1). When you feel you know what you are doing, use this chart to see what needs to be given an energy bath in your life. You will be amazed how much better you will feel after clearing a space, whether in your house or car.

If you run into negative energy or a discarnate being (a ghost), do not fear. Call on Archangel Michael and his helpers to clear the space. Sometimes in your mind's eye you can see the angels assisting negative thought forms or discarnate beings away from your space. Sometimes, too, you may need to call on Jesus and Mary, two of the world's great healers.

You can even clear energy in an office or a hospital. One time a friend asked me to clear a hospital because her uncle was so bothered by the discarnate beings, who had gotten stuck between worlds and were hanging around at the hospital. When I began the clearing, I could see in my mind's eye busloads of people leaving the hospital. There were a few stragglers that the angels had to help because they were afraid of going to the other side. But with the aid of Michael's assistants, they too left. When I checked on my friend's uncle, he put his hand on his heart, smiled, and took a peaceful nap. He passed a few days later.

After doing a major clearing, you might also notice you are a little tired, maybe exhausted. It can take some psychic energy, so just allow yourself time to rest.

- Who needs to be cleared? If another person, you need to ask psychically for permission. Just say, "Do I have your permission to clear you?" If the answer is *no*, then you can pray for them.

- What needs to be cleared?

- Is there anything else?

Feelings (Chart 17)

(See page 197.)

Becoming aware of our feelings and what they are communicating to us is a lifelong practice. Sometimes feelings can become intense, and we seem out of control. At other times they are nagging and won't let us be at peace.

Just getting to know our feelings and respecting them is a process that we perhaps should all be taught in elementary school. When you're angry, it means someone or something is unfair. When you're sad, it means you have lost something important to you, whether it be an object or a friend.

Unfortunately, we, especially boys, are taught to suppress our feelings. Don't get too angry, upset, mad, or sad! And, just like on television, we learn we're supposed to be happy. Wouldn't it be easier if we didn't have feelings or at least so many of them? Unfortunately, ignoring them just doesn't seem to work. They tend to intensify and surface at the most inconvenient moments, and out pops an overly angry word or sentence that, when calm, we would have never wanted to say to our best friend.

Rumi, the poet and mystic, teaches us to welcome our feelings, all of them. In his famous poem "The Guest House," he writes:

This being human is a guest house.
Every morning a new arrival.
A joy, a depression, a meanness,
some momentary awareness comes
as an unexpected visitor.
Welcome and entertain them all!

Of course, this is a daily and lifelong process.

This Feelings Chart is to help you recognize your feelings. After you have experienced them and asked them what their message is, perhaps through journaling and talking with a friend, you can ask the chart, "What would feel better?" Then you can choose a positive feeling and write an affirmation for yourself.

- What am I feeling right now? (Feelings Chart)

- What else am I feeling? (Feelings Chart)

- What other feeling(s) might make me feel better? (Feelings Chart)

- What else do I need? (Table of Charts/Human Needs Chart)

Human Needs (Chart 18)

(See page 199.)

Needs (are) at the roots of feelings.

—MARSHALL B. ROSENBERG, Ph.D.,
Nonviolent Communication: A Language of Life

Use this chart in conjunction with the Feelings Chart (17), so that after you figure out what you're feeling, you can discover what you need.

Use this chart to quickly get to the heart of what, for you, is essential.

Sometimes communicating what you require can be frightening. Sometimes the world judges us for asking for what we truly want. Sometimes women are taught they're supposed to take care of everyone else and not have needs.

After all these years, I am still learning to express my needs and desires. I often go into child mode when asking. In my family of origin, we were not supposed to express feelings or needs. So, still today, I'm a little scared to ask.

I never do it perfectly. But I am learning and growing. I often have a back-up plan just in case the person I ask can't meet my needs. I always remind myself that I will certainly have a much better chance of having my needs met if I ask. Yes, it's so simple, yet sometimes still difficult. Keep on practicing.

- What do I truly need?

- What else would help?

- What would solve the problem?

Self-Care (Chart 19)

(See page 201.)

When I was a mother with two small children and running a company, I underwent counseling after experiencing panic attacks. I was told I needed to take care of myself and that included exercise, meditation, and time to relax. I admit that, at the time, I was just amazed by the concept of self-care. I needed to be given permission to nurture myself. I learned that if I didn't care for myself, I wouldn't be able to take care of my children, my home, or my business. What a concept.

When all is too busy and spinning, the best thing you can do is take a time-out and practice giving to yourself. This chart gives you multiple ways to reinvigorate your life. Use the pendulum to see what you truly need. In addition, here is another short list of ways to be kind and take care of yourself.

Write a new affirmation on a card and say it throughout the day.

Start a compliments box and write down sweet things others say to you.

Go cloud watching; lie on the grass, ground, or sand if you can; and breathe deeply.

Take one-minute meditations between activities and say your affirmation.

Do a mini-declutter of a bookshelf, drawer, or closet. Give something away to someone as a gift.

Go to a dance, aerobics, or yoga class. Pretend you're sixteen.

Stretch, walk, or jog in your nearest park. Hug a tree.

Ask your body what it wants and listen. Then do that.

Give yourself the gift of a massage, pedicure, or manicure.

Eat your veggies, drink water, and love yourself.

See the beauty in birds, animals, plants, and trees.

Watch the flames in a fire, and cuddle with a cat or friend.

Cook and enjoy a healthy, delicious meal with family or friends.

Attend a live music performance or play, and soak in the richness.

Find and give yourself time to read a great book.

- What do I need to do for myself?

- What would I like to do for myself?

- What else would help?

Healing Arts (Chart 20)

(See page 203.)

Today we can see many different types of healing professionals if we are having health challenges. From counselors to physicians to shamans, we can choose those who will help us on our journey.

Many times, we need to create a healing team to help us through a difficult illness. Use this chart to see who and what would be of benefit to you. Look to those who give you solutions, hope, and a positive outlook to face your issues—perhaps a traditional and holistic doctor for the body, a therapist for the mind, and a minister or psychic healer for the spirit, as well as lots of friends and family with love and support for you.

Here are descriptions of some of the healing modalities included on the Healing Arts Chart you might not be familiar with:

- **Acupuncture** is a form of alternative medicine in which thin needles are inserted into energy points on the body to aid in healing.

- **Aromatherapy** (also known as essential oil therapy) is the art, science, and practice of using the essence of aromatic plants for mental and physical health.

- **Ayurveda** is an ancient, traditional Hindu system of medicine, which is based on the idea of balance in bodily systems; it uses diet, herbal treatment, and yogic breathing.

- **Chinese Medicine** originated in ancient China and has evolved over thousands of years. Practitioners use herbal medicines and various mind and body practices, such as acupuncture and tai chi, to treat or prevent health problems.[26]

- **Chiropractic** is a system of complementary medicine based on the diagnosis and manipulative treatment of misalignments of the joints, especially those of the spinal column, which are considered to cause other disorders by affecting the nerves, muscles, and organs.

- **Crystal Healing** is an alternative therapy where stones and crystals are placed on the chakras or near the body to promote balance and well-being.

- **Emotional Freedom Technique (EFT) Tapping** was founded by Gary Craig. It is a form of energy psychology in which a person taps along nine meridian points of the body in order to confront limiting beliefs. EFT can be effective for emotional healing.

....

[26] National Center for Complementary and Integrative Health, "Traditional Chinese Medicine: In Depth," October 2013, https://nccih.nih.gov/health/whatiscam/chinesemed.htm.

- **Flower Essences** are herbal infusions or decoctions, made from the flowering part of the plant, which uniquely address emotional, mental, and soul aspects of wellness.[27]

- **Healing Codes** are a simple and powerful self-healing system and a form of energy medicine. They were discovered in 2001 by Alex Loyd, PhD, ND.[28]

- **Magnetic Therapy** uses magnets for healing and pain relief.

- **Naturopathy** is a system of medicine based on the healing power of nature. Naturopathy is a holistic system, meaning that naturopathic doctors (ND) or naturopathic medical doctors (NMD) strive to find the cause of disease by understanding the body, mind, and spirit of the person.

- **Naturopathic Doctors** rely on natural methods of healing, helping the body to heal itself. They use homeopathy, herbs, and acupuncture.

- **Reiki** is a Japanese technique for stress reduction and relaxation that also promotes healing. It is administered by a "laying on of hands" and is based on the idea that an unseen "life force energy" flows through us and is what animates our being.

- **Shamanism** is an ancient system regarded as having access to, and influence in, the world of good and evil spirits, especially practiced among some peoples of northern Asia and North and South America. Typically, shamans enter a trance state during a ritual, and practice divination and healing.

---

[27] Flower Essence Services, "What Are Flower Essences," *www.fesflowers.com/product-info/flower-essences/what-are-flower-essences/*.

[28] Alex Loyd, "Your Healthiest, Happiest & Most Successful Life," *www.dralexanderloyd.com/*.

- **Sound Healing** has been used for thousands of years to help people heal. It can be used to help people meditate, reduce stress, and make lifestyle changes.

- **Spiritual Response Therapy (SRT)** is a spiritual-energetic approach to health and well-being, which offers a radical new way to clear the template of the body, upon which our physical, mental, and emotional health depends. Through intention and focused awareness, a remote energetic connection takes place in SRT, which then allows the practitioner to do clearing work. The work is done in an altered state, using a pendulum and a set of charts, to find and clear negative energies and soul programming that is blocking a person's well-being at all levels.

- **Therapeutic Touch** is a systematic approach to the age-old laying on of hands to help people reduce anxiety, relax, and aid in the healing process.

- What healing professional do I need to see?

- Who else could help me?

- What else would help me?

- Who would I like to help me?

Foods (Chart 21)

(See page 205.)

I've included this chart so that you can check to see if you are eating the right foods. It's a complicated subject, and there are many schools of thought. If it feels overwhelming, you can go to a healthcare provider or nutritionist who will help you make the right choices. This was key for me when I was pregnant.

You can also test your food by holding it in one hand and the pendulum in the other. Ask: "What is the positive? What is the negative?" using the Time and Percent Chart (2).

- What does my body need?

- What else does it need?

- Will this food help me?

Vitamins and Minerals (Chart 22)

(See page 207.)

The facts are in: a healthy diet is your best option for receiving all your nutritional needs. Your healthcare professional can advise you. Then use this chart when you wish to know if you need a vitamin or supplement.

You can also test supplements by holding them in one hand and the pendulum in the other. Ask: "What is the positive? What is the negative?" using the Time and Percent Chart (2). You will feel the energy when a vitamin, mineral, or even a beauty product is good for you.

- What does my body need?

- What else does it need?

- Will this help me?

- How much will this help?

- What is the positive? [Use the Time and Percent Chart (2) to get the positive and negative score.]

- What is the negative? [Use the Time and Percent Chart (2) to get the positive and negative score.]

Flower Essences (Chart 23)

(See page 209.)

Flower essences are energetic remedies and herbal infusions used primarily for emotional healing and stress release. They are a therapy for the soul that works to strengthen a person emotionally, mentally, and spiritually in order to learn life's lessons. Not a cure-all, they work well in conjunction with other healing modalities.

After working in traditional medicine and with homeopathy, Dr. Edward Bach, a British physician, concluded that disease was created over time by disharmony, unhappy thoughts, and feelings. In 1930, he left his medical practice to search for a cure in which the whole person was addressed. Bach then later rediscovered the healing properties of flowers and how to use them with his patients. He intuitively created thirty-eight essences, all of which grew within walking distance of his home. Today he is regarded as the first creator of modern day flower essences.

In 1980, Richard Katz and Patricia Kaminski created the Flower Essence Society (FES) to research, gather case studies, and confirm the positive effects of flower essences. They first studied Bach flower essences and later created their own line of flower essences, called Quintessentials, from organic flowers grown in the Sierra Nevada Mountains of California. While Bach's flower essences are used primarily to treat unhappiness and depression, the FES Quintessentials are used primarily to help people develop spiritually, release blocks to creativity, and improve relationships.

Richard and Patricia also teach and conduct classes worldwide. They have a well-researched quarterly journal and are the authors of the *Flower Essence Repertory*, a flower essence "bible" with detailed information on Bach and Californian flower essences. From this book you can learn, research, and prescribe essences that will help you on your healing journey. There are no adverse side effects of flower essences. For more information, see *www.flowersociety.org*.

For those wanting to know more about flower essences and aromatherapy, I highly recommend *Flower Power* by Anne McIntyre.[29] McIntyre is described as a "green, wise woman" with much compassion and understanding of flower remedies. Her book inspires flower lovers and awakens a new understanding of the flowers' power to heal.

Patricia Kaminski offers this information on making flower essences: "To make your own flower essences, keep in mind that you are looking for a pristine plant community of the flower you wish to prepare. This population of plants should be at the peak expression in its annual flowering, to ensure that you are tapping into the Cosmic Archetype that is flowing into the plant from higher dimensions. Also Dr. Bach's method involves a precise confluence of the four elements that weave around the plant's life matrix: earth, air, water and sun (warmth). Therefore you will be setting the bowl on the earth where the plant is growing in a clean and harmonious environment. This will need to be done in the open air on a clear, unpolluted day, using pure and vibrant water from the local region of the plant. The flowers are collected in the early morning as the sun is rising with the process concluded in approximately three to four hours as the sun reaches its high point in the heavens. Always begin the process by asking permission and making connection with the Spiritual/Elemental identity of the plant and the Divine Creative Forces that have brought it into Being. Keep your soul gently connected and lovingly aware of this spiritual reality while the flower medicine is being prepared.

"After a few hours, you can use your pendulum to ask if the archetypal essence of the flower is fully infused in the water. Give thanks again for the opportunity to use the flowers for a soul medicine. You can then strain off the plant substance and preserve the liquid "mother" matrix with pure organic brandy, apple cider vinegar, or glycerin. This mother substance can then be diluted several drops at a time into water and used in a spray or dropper bottle or added to massage oils or other

---

[29] Anne McIntyre, *Flower Power* (New York, NY: Henry Holt & Company, Inc., 1996).

similar healing preparations. Do all with loving care, and you will have an emotional and spiritual medicine for yourself and loved ones."

For this chart, I picked thirty-four essences using my pendulum.

- What flower essence would be good for my happiness?

- What flower essence would be good for healing?

- What flower essence would help my spirit?

- Is there another essence that would enhance my overall well-being?

Aromatherapy (Chart 24)

(See page 211.)

Aromatherapy, also referred to as essential oil therapy, extracts aromatic essences from plants and is used for healing. Most ancient civilizations had a long history using aromatic oils to enhance baths, massages, and for inhalations to aid in healing.

In 1910, French perfumer and chemist René-Maurice Gattefossé (1881-1950) was experimenting in his laboratory when he accidentally burned his hand. He plunged the injured hand into the nearest vat of liquid, which happened to be a vat of essential oil of lavender. Amazed at how quickly the wound healed and at the minimal scarring—much less than he anticipated—he was inspired to study other essential oils. His book, *Gattefossé's Aromatherapy*, was published in 1937. Gattefossé coined the term *aromatherapy*.

For years I worked with a knowledgeable woman who, after a short counseling session to discover my primary emotional issues, used a pendulum to dowse her aromatherapy and flower essence kits for the right remedies. She would make me a spray bottle with spring water and the essences. It was to be used two or three times a day for the next few weeks for self-healing. Such a gift! And yes, I moved through many of my emotional and spiritual issues with help from the flowers.

Aromatherapy is such a fascinating and powerful healing tool. You can do this for yourself or find a trained healer in your area to help you.

You do have to be careful with essential oils, though, as they are highly concentrated substances. Small amounts work best, a few drops diluted in spring water or oil. Go slowly. Most are for external use only and cannot be used around the eyes and ear canal. Check with your health food store herbalist, healer, or doctor.

I have included thirty essential oils helpful to readers.

• What scent am I attracted to?

• What scent could help heal me?

• What other scent do I need?

Crystals (Chart 25)

(See page 213.)

It is fitting that as I write I am sitting next to my bowl of crystals and my large magic wand. The wand is made of a crystal ball at one end, with purple leather on the rod, and a clear quartz crystal at the other end. One sharp crystal is used to cut away that which is no longer necessary, such as negative thoughts or beliefs, and one crystal to empower the subtle senses of clairvoyance (seeing) and clairaudience (hearing).

I would not call myself an expert on crystals, but somehow, over the years, crystals have come to me. I received an amethyst at the birth of my daughter and a few I've purchased to commemorate new beginnings, such as starting a business. I also used them for healing during a particularly difficult breakup with a fiancé.

I've collected crystals from where I lived in Brazil years ago. Some came from a friend who lived in Arkansas, whose house was built over a vein of crystals. When I moved from my home in Boulder Creek, I found them in every nook and cranny of our house. After I moved into my loft at the Tannery Arts, I put them in an old Italian bowl that had belonged to my father. There all the crystals sit, happy to be together. Clients pick them up and soak up the energy. I place them in the sun and occasionally wash them in salt water. I love them and consider them to be precious gifts from our Divine Mother Earth.

Over the years, they have become my stone friends, yet I was still learning more about them while researching this book. Medicine people and shamans have used crystals for centuries for increasing their power and healing their patients. Today, they are still used by spiritual healers and massage therapists for clearing, healing, and raising a person's vibration. You can use them for focusing energy and as aids in meditation. There are also stones that correspond to the chakras; as a self-healing practice, you can lie down and place them on each of your chakras. Usually, the color of the stone and the color of the chakra will correspond.

As you first learn about crystals, it's good to keep it simple. You can use this chart and ask what crystal would be helpful to you. Then you can visit your local rock and crystal shop to see what attracts you. You can take your pendulum and practice dowsing at the store if you feel comfortable.

You can hold a crystal in your hand and ask the spirit of the crystal: "What is your purpose? Could we be allies? How could I work with you?" You will notice that different crystals have different vibrations and voices—some soft and healing, and others more energetic and powerful. You can feel the difference between rose quartz (used to heal the heart) and smoky quartz (used to protect and ground).

I dowsed for what crystals would be helpful to readers of this book. Please feel free to add your own favorites to the chart. Enjoy your new journey with your crystal friends.

- What crystal would be helpful to my mind, my body, or my soul?

- Is there another crystal that could address this issue?

- What crystal could I buy for my day-to-day well-being?

CHAPTER 7

Transitions, Endings, and
New Beginnings Charts

Death is no more than passing from one room into
another. But there's a difference for me, you know.
Because in that other room I shall be able to see.

—HELEN KELLER

The really hard part of life occurs when we truly learn we are not in charge. We often have to surrender to the experience of a transition we didn't necessarily want—such as loss of a job or illness or the death of a loved one. In the process we have to find a way to forgive those in our past and ourselves so that if someone dies, we are at peace with them. And it's so necessary to let your loved ones know how you love and care for them.

I had to learn that death is not the enemy, but instead a rather stern but necessary teacher. Death also could be an ally to those in pain and anguish, by taking the suffering loved ones home.

Death taught me that life is short and we must not put off whatever we wish to do. The impact of my mother's death made me decide I had to find what I really loved doing in life.

I knew I needed to listen to my inner self and live a different life. I spent a good year asking myself and the universe, "What am I supposed to be doing with my life?" Yes, the universe answered. In a year I was in a new relationship with my soon-to-be husband and with an exciting new company that supported my family for twenty-five years.

I learned it was important not to waste time on anything I didn't truly find essential.

Remember, as you go through the many transitions in your life, let go and let your intuition guide you. No matter how turbulent the waters, you will find yourself taken care of and in new, unexpected, but abundant rivers of life.

Stages of Grief and Healing (Chart 26)

(See page 215.)

When you're going through profound grief, it can be good to know and acknowledge the stages of grief and healing. You should know and be reassured you are not different, that what you are experiencing is part of the process of healing. The ground beneath you has shifted or given way, and you are in a new process of finding yourself once again.

Love and patience for yourself are absolutely necessary. Know that the feelings of grief and loss will lessen over time. Seek out friends, counselors, or grief groups for support. You will recover—love and time are the great healers.

- **Shock:** A feeling that occurs when you first learn of an illness, whether yours or another's, or during the death of a friend or family member. You just feel as if a hole has been blown into your chest.

- **Denial:** A feeling that this is not happening. You just can't believe it, and you refuse to acknowledge the reality.

- **Anger:** A furious feeling that life, death, and God are playing with you, and it's not fair, just, or good.

- **Bargaining:** An attempt to talk God into a different plan. *Take me, not him.*

- **Depression:** A numbed-out feeling, anger internalized; it's really hard to get out of bed, show up for other people, work, or do life.

- **Acceptance:** Though you can't change anything, you finally accept the truth of the situation.

- **Rebirth:** A time of renewal and energy. Still rocky but you are headed for happier days.

- **New Life:** Though a sad or shocking event has taken place, you decide to move forward and embrace your new life.

You can go through different stages in random order. Just when you think you have processed all the feelings, people, events, and geography can trigger you. And you will feel you are reprocessing all the same feelings over and over again. Let yourself feel and let go. Let the angels surround and comfort you. Know you are loved. This too shall pass, and you will feel better, or different, soon.

- What stage of healing am I in?

- What other stage am I experiencing?

Letting Go and Death (Chart 27)

(See page 217.)

Before my husband's death, I visited a psychic, who told me "Death is a teacher for you in this lifetime." At the time I was grieving the loss of my current life. I knew my husband was dying; the angels had told me so from the beginning of his illness. In her wise woman voice, she said, "Though you don't know it now, you shall recover. In time you will even receive new gifts."

At the time this wasn't really what I wanted to hear. I still wanted my nuclear family back. I wanted our mornings together as a family, getting ready for school and work, the dog and cats fed, and dinners around the dining room table. We lived in a beautiful old-fashioned coral-colored house on the San Lorenzo River in Boulder Creek, California, beneath towering hundred-foot redwood trees. When we got home from our busy day, we all got in the hot tub together, where we talked about our day. We were fortunate. We were blessed.

But all of that suddenly changed! Every morning I woke up to the fact that my husband was dying. I was terrified to go into his room. Perhaps something had happened to him in the night. I wanted my life back in the worst way, especially the warm feeling that everything was going to be fine.

By the time my husband died, he had gone through multiple operations, chemotherapy, and radiation; he was just a shadow of his former self. I knew that when he passed he was going to a better place and that he would be out of pain, loss, and trauma. I knew he would be restored to his funny, bright, and intelligent self.

The night he died and the day afterwards as he lay in the morgue before he was cremated, I worried about his body. I wanted to run to the morgue and make sure he had plenty of blankets and air to breathe. I knew my thoughts were irrational. I had another level of letting go to experience. I had to totally surrender him to God and the angels who would take care of him.

At the time I felt like an injured bird that could no longer fly, but I had to show a sunnier side to the world. I had children in elementary school to raise and a high-tech marketing company to run. I truly don't know how I did it. I spent time daily grieving in my car on the way to work. It was my only time alone. I had help from counselors and friends. My children and animals were a great comfort. I had much to live for.

If you have suffered a great loss, know that you will heal. It will take days, weeks, months, and years. It will take as long as is needed. Grief cannot be rushed and, like ocean waves that rise, fall, and meet the shore, your grief will lessen over time.

Moving through an illness or the death of a loved one is an aspect of life that we must all face. At times the process can seem like a harsh, painful teacher. Yet this is a time—if we allow it—for the pain to open our hearts so that we may find inner resources of courage, faith, forgiveness, and love—resources that perhaps we did not know we even possessed.

It is a time to complete and say goodbye, to thank those in our lives that have made a difference. It's a time to clean up any issues in relationships, a time to say all those things in your heart, and a time to forgive old hurts. It's a time to bless loved ones and children, a time to let regret go, and a time to give thanks to the life that gave us so much.

We all die. Our bodies die and our spirits live on. In my psychic healings, I have met many of my clients' loved ones who are on the other side and come with messages for their friends and relatives. I am amazed by the specificity and details that are offered that have rich meaning for my clients. From these experiences I have every assurance that we do survive after life.

Since the advent of, and advances in, modern medicine, many people are revived close to or after death. Today, there are many accounts and books on near-death experiences. I have read and reread over the years how these stories describe the peace of an afterlife that many have experienced and come back to report.

Fear of the unknown can lessen as we learn more about the dying process. It's an intense and meaningful time when a loved one dies. You will deal with many emotions and states of being, perhaps even guilt. Above all, be sure to be loving and kind to yourself.

This chart's tools offer solace and hope through the illness, grieving, and dying process, whether it is for a loved one or ourselves. Use what comforts and works best for you.

- What is needed?

- What am I afraid of?

- What do I need to complete?

Life Transitions (Chart 28)

(See page 219.)

It seems that my whole life has been about change, so many transitions. When I was a child, my family moved all the time because my father was a custom homebuilder in the San Francisco Bay Area. We moved to a new home every three years, often in a new town. I was used to packing boxes. One of my earliest memories is of picking up my sand toys from our second house because we were moving. In some ways it's hard for me not to move, not to have a new place to live every three years. Now I redecorate my loft apartment to satisfy my need for change.

Change in life comes in all forms—physical, mental, emotional, and spiritual. We are not a finished person, but an ongoing experiment in living; what works at one time in life may not work later on. We are always changing, growing, shrinking, stepping out and then back into life, forever morphing—and so our lives reflect these changes.

If transitions are consciously unwelcome or abrupt, such as an illness or a chronic condition, we can find ourselves suddenly having to adapt. Our first inclination is most probably to resist. With time to reflect, take action, and learn, we can once more flow with life and its changes. We will, even if we don't want to, most probably grow emotionally and spiritually. Perhaps unexpectedly, opportunities will materialize out of the new reality. When we find ourselves between doors of opportunity, it is important to remember this situation will not last forever and that we have many choices.

This is an excellent time to use the pendulum and this chart to maneuver your way through difficult transitions.

- What do I need?

- What do I want?

- How do I get out of the hallway, this in-between place?

- Where is the window? Where is the door?

- What is next?

Gratitude (Chart 29)

(See page 221.)

Often in the midst of a busy life or a crisis, we can forget to be grateful, to show appreciation for what we already have. Gratitude can shift a sad or angry moment by helping us remember all that we do have—how rich we truly are in life. After journaling in the morning, I love writing a gratitude list. There is so much to appreciate if I only take the time to notice.

If I'm upset, I challenge myself to write a list until I feel a bit better. I start with my cat, the birds, refreshing air, trees, plants, flowers, my adult children, and all the wonderful people in my life. I count my blessings. Sometimes if I'm perturbed in traffic or waiting in line at the grocery store, I mentally write a gratitude list. I also try to breathe and remember to be patient. (I'm still working on this quality.)

Remember there are many benefits to being grateful. Gratitude makes us happier and healthier. There have been numerous studies documenting this fact. For more information, go to *happierhuman.com/the-science-of-gratitude/*.

I included this chart to remind us that we all have much to be thankful for in our lives. Add your own words from your gratitude lists. (You can use the chart to discover what new blessings Spirit could bring into your life.)

- What do I have now in my life that I am grateful for?

- What else could I be grateful for?

- What would I like to bring into my life?

Healthy Living (Chart 30)

(See page 223.)

I liked writing the Healthy Living Chart because it's good to remember to keep it simple. Life is not about perfection, but about growing and embracing positive change, becoming a little better every day. After reading numerous books on healing, I have come to the conclusion that if we follow some fundamental guidelines developed by medical doctors and health professionals, we can have the greatest gift of all—health.

I urge you to give up bad habits (that ice cream sundae *every* night?) and let go of addictions that might be quickly or slowly killing you (alcohol or smoking?). Giving up these habits sounds so easy, but it can be so difficult. With help, it is possible though. In class yesterday, I said, "No, it's not that hard." A class member had an awakening. Embrace your new freedom to choose a healthy, spirit-filled life. Love life and share your best self with others. It's not always easy, but, with support, the reward is good health.

An encouraging book is Dr. Maoshing Ni's *Secrets of Longevity: Hundreds of Ways to Live to Be 100*. Just the title is inspiring. The book offers ideas about food, healing, environment, exercise, and life in general. After I read the food section, I ran to the grocery store to buy ingredients and try out the healthy suggestions. From a Chinese herb to benefit your hair and scalp to help for arthritis sufferers, this book is worth its weight in gold.

Most of us were born healthy. If we can live in a clean environment, eat well, exercise, and be connected to others and Spirit, we have an opportunity to be well. Don't forget to sleep, find a job you love, and give to others.

Check this chart to give yourself a health checkup.

- What am I doing right?

- What could I be doing better?

- Does any area of healthy living need my attention right now?

CHAPTER 8

Other Pendulum Exercises

The wound is the place where the Light enters you.

—RUMI

In this chapter we will look at other ways we can use the pendulum and Intuitive Healing Charts. Many of these exercises came to me intuitively as I worked with the SRT charts and my own charts. As you begin using the Intuitive Healing Charts, you will also be led to new ways to use the pendulum and charts. Some of these may seem pretty far out. Well, yes, they are!

I was brought up in a Christian home, attended Sunday school, and later developed a personal relationship with Jesus and Mary Magdalene while studying the Unity teachings, *A Course in Miracles*, and Paramahansa Yogananda's writings. I somewhat believed in some sort of afterlife and reincarnation, but it wasn't until I experienced actually talking with people who had died that my belief and knowledge were strengthened.

After a long day of work, children tucked in finally, it was strange to be in my bedroom and find myself conversing with my late husband, who had passed away two years before. At that stage his death was still very painful, as I was coming out of deep grief. These and other experiences with my late husband and others helped me understand that, yes, there is physical death, but our souls go on to another realm, a place where they can still communicate with us on earth.

A second belief that was strengthened for me after working the charts was that many of us have lived many lives. Some people have had just a few lives, and others have been here many times. Who has not heard a wise person described as an "old soul"?

A third belief I now hold is that, by clearing our traumatic past lives, we can become free of old values, anxieties, fears, and phobias that have plagued us in this life. We might have gone to traditional therapy for months or years attempting to let go of thoughts and beliefs that never served us, but to no avail. By using the charts, visualization, imagination, and clearing, we can access our past lives, which gives us a deeper understanding and compassion for ourselves. "Oh, I understand now why I don't trust men (or women)" or "I understand why I don't like water (or forests or the mountains)" or "I understand now why I am so passionate about my work." Doing this research on past lives can clear up many mysteries about yourself and your relationships. Also, it can release hidden talents from past lives. That, in itself, can be rewarding.

By using the pendulum and the Intuitive Healing Charts, over time you will just naturally expand your consciousness and powers. For some, it will be hearing the still, small voice of Spirit. For others, it may be seeing in your mind's eye angels, spirit helpers, or Spirit Guides. You may see pictures or mini-movies about past lives. For others, it may be a strong intuition or a feeling in your body. (You just know what is right for yourself.)

How can we feel limited when we can explore the depths of others and ourselves with the pendulum and the charts?

PAST LIVES

If you're feeling too old, remember that in truth you are ancient and most probably have lived many lives, perhaps thousands. So what is forty, fifty, or sixty-five years young? This is fun—you can ask using the pendulum and charts how many past lives you have lived on earth. How old are you really?

Go to the Time and Percent Chart (2) and ask:

- How many earth lives have I had?

- How many as a woman? A man?

- How many as a healer, a shaman, a doctor, a lawyer, etc.?

HOW TO COMMUNICATE WITH A DECEASED LOVED ONE

The process of communicating with a deceased loved one is for people who feel comfortable with their dowsing skills and who are curious about whom they can connect with on the other side. For me, this ability naturally appeared, but over the years I have taught others how to contact and connect with their loved ones.

When I travel inwardly, I work with the angels of light and love, the archangels, Jesus, and Mary. You can ask them to guide your journey or request another spirit guide that you are comfortable with. I have never had a problem when I know Archangel Michael (for protection) and Archangel Gabriel (for communication) are with me.

I do this communication either in my meditation chair or in my bed before sleep. I do a short centering meditation and pray asking, "Please angels, Jesus, and Mary, be with me as I contact _____." Clear yourself, and then just sit quietly and breathe. Have your charts open to the Feelings Chart (17).

I practiced this type of communication recently with my wonderful mother, Barbara Jean Torvik, who died many years ago. I took a few moments and saw her in my mind's eye. (Or you could use a picture of your loved one.) I had this conversation with her:

"Hi, Mom. It's so good to spend time with you." I see her sparkling, clear blue eyes.

"I'm so proud of you. I've been rooting for you. You just keep on writing and painting."

"Mom, how is heaven?"

"Heavenly. I just can be myself. There is no stress. I am recovering and still learning from my experience in Earth School. Now, I am resting, healing, and creating."

"Are you happy?" This is my concern. She had a hard life on earth.

"Yes, yes, no need to worry. Please stop. It doesn't help. I'm painting too. Just like you. It's just different. We paint in many dimensions. You will understand when you come home."

"Are you going to reincarnate soon?"

"No. I'm taking a longer break."

"Will I see you when I go home to heaven?"

"Yes, of course."

"Will you still be there?"

"Yes."

"I miss you." (I shed a few tears. It's been so long—thirty-three years.) "I still feel this strong connection with you, Mom. I'm so glad you're well."

Then I checked the charts to confirm my feelings and hers. The Feelings Chart for me indicated "blessed, connected, and joy." For my mother, the words were "beautiful and inspired."

One more time I returned to the Table of Charts and asked, "Is there anything else?" The pendulum pointed to the Flower Essences Chart (23), and on the chart were the words "wild rose." Then I heard my mother in my mind's ear say, "You are my beautiful wild rose."

It's so sweet to connect with loved ones. Enjoy the comforting and reassuring presence of your loved ones on the other side.

HOW TO CLEAR DECEASED LOVED ONES

In the days that followed my husband's death, I felt a door had slammed shut. It was such a mystery about where he had gone. Other friends were having psychic experiences with him, but I hadn't yet.

When I began using the SRT Charts, he came to me quickly and asked me if I would clear him. I heard him say that he still felt drugged from the anti-seizure medication, chemotherapy, radiation, and surgery. Before he was sick, he was a smart and funny man. He wanted his clarity and sense of humor back. I was so grateful to have a way in which to help him.

When you clear a person on the other side, you do it the same way as if that person were physically in front of you. First, you ask their permission. "Do I have your permission to clear you?" When you receive a *yes* answer, proceed.

Then ask Archangel Raphael to help, or Jesus and Mary. Say, "Please clear them of any and all illnesses, drugs, surgeries, and procedures from their last earthly life that may prevent them from having a fulfilling journey." If the person had a long or painful transition, clearing may take a little while. You can also ask the angels to continue clearing and healing your loved ones as you go about your day. Clearing, healing, and prayers help those on the other side very much.

HOW TO CLEAR AND COMMUNICATE WITH ANIMALS

Yes, you can clear your pets, just as you would clear a person. First, ask their permission. Then, if the pendulum indicates *yes*, which it usually does (because animals like feeling clear just as we do), let your pendulum move in a circular pattern until they are cleared. They will be curious about what you are doing. My cat likes to bat the pendulum around.

You can also do a quick body scan by slowly moving the pendulum over your pet's body, making sure energetically everything is well with their body. Your pendulum will start moving in a clockwise motion when anything needs clearing. Just let the pendulum do its work.

You can also use the charts to communicate with your animals. You can ask them how they are feeling using the Feelings Chart (17). And ask them if they need anything from you, using the Human Needs Chart

(18). Communicating with your animals can be rewarding, and it can help you to know what they need.

My friend Mike called me frantically to tell me his dog was sick and most probably dying. He asked me to go with him to his vet to put his dog to sleep. I knew his dog, a smart Sheltie, and knew he wasn't ordinary, rather a communicative, intuitive dog, very bonded with his owner and vice versa. This special dog had seen Mike through some dark days after his wife died.

Of course, I went to the veterinarian and later spent the whole day with Mike. When we left the vet's office, the dog was out of his physical body and out of pain—now a spirit dog. He just followed us out of the office and hopped in the back seat. I could clearly see and hear him. The dog didn't understand why Mike was so upset. All day long I acted as an intermediary, facilitating communication between the two. As the day went on, my friend gradually felt better. I told him it would be good to feed his dog some dry food, as the dog wouldn't really understand why he wasn't being fed.

A month later, Mike called me sad and upset. He didn't know why he was having this emotional reaction. When I asked and looked clair-voyantly, I saw that his dog was attempting to get Mike's attention to say goodbye so that he could go to the light. I let Mike know that it was time to let go and release his dog so that he could continue on his journey. Mike grieved, but then in two weeks, we visited the Humane Society in Monterey, where he found another dog who needed a home. I have never seen such a happy meeting between an owner and a dog—it was more like a reunion between old friends who hadn't seen each other in ages.

Yes, animals have souls, and yes, we can communicate with them. They remind us of our humanness and how to love and be kind to all creatures.

HOW TO INVESTIGATE AND CLEAR A PAST LIFE WITH OTHERS

When I was in my early thirties, curious about who I was, I had a past life regression with a hypnotherapist. She was a friend of a friend, and I immediately felt comfortable with her, as if I had met her before. She had a gentle and loving spirit. In a dimly lit room, she sat next to me in a chair, as I lay on a couch and was taken on a journey to my past lives. In the guided visualization, I became more and more relaxed as I floated and traveled. Part of me let go and followed her simple instructions.

Then she instructed me that I was going to visit my first past life. I was to gently float down into my shoes of the first past life. I looked down and saw distinctly the shoes of that life and then, in my mind's eye, a little movie of that life.

In another life, my husband and I were hardy settlers living in a remote cabin on top of a mountain in Colorado in the 1800s. Then in the past life reading, I discovered that during our past life tragedy had struck while we were living in a little cabin on the mountaintop. I was pregnant at the time, and right after my husband left to buy supplies, the baby came early. When he returned home, he found I had died in childbirth.

In my current life, my ex-boyfriend and I had many adventures; we lived in San Francisco and bought five acres outside of Nevada City a few miles up the mountain, but close to town. We built a small house together and also lived part-time in Brazil. My ex-boyfriend didn't want to get married or have children. We had other differences that I never understood because we were so close and had a great life together. After the reading, I felt I could much more easily forgive him and myself. Today, this ex-boyfriend still owns the little house that we built. I have always loved the mountains, but I like to stay close to town. When I have to go up winding mountains to the peak, I still get anxious and feel better when I am further down the mountain.

During the course of this reading, I visited five past lives. Each one of them helped me see a bigger picture of myself and helped explain my past romantic relationships. I realized that the people in my current life were playing different or similar roles as in past lives. Afterwards, I spent the day and evening in an altered state. The experience gave me a totally different feeling about reincarnation and myself.

Years ago I began doing readings and healings for clients, and when I cleared their chakras, I started seeing symbols in my mind's eye, little movies about my clients' past lives; sometimes to my astonishment, weapons—knives, axes, and machetes—were stuck in their chakras.

By clearing past lives, you release the past. You are then ready for a full life. Pain and blocks from the past are gone. The gifts of a past life can now be brought into the present life. Often we don't know why we can't clear a health challenge. By using the Intuitive Healing Charts and pendulum, you can investigate.

Sometimes we may be held back by a challenge with another person from this life or a past life. We don't know why a relationship that should be better isn't. When you clear the past, suddenly that relationship can become easier. You can approach it with a more understanding attitude.

You can clear the roles you played in a past life. For example, you might have had several lives where you were sister and brother, or wife and husband. If you're in a relationship and having problems with sex, you might want to clear any sister/brother roles from a past life. After all, in the past life, just as it is today, it was considered taboo to have sexual thoughts or relations with your sister or brother.

You can use this exercise to clear. Remember to ground and center yourself. You can research past lives using the pendulum and the charts by asking:

- Did I have a past life with this person? [Yes/No and Clearing Signal Chart (1)]

- Is this a past life issue with this person? [Yes/No and Clearing Signal Chart (1)]

- How many lives did I have with this person? [Time and Percent Chart (2)]

- How was this person related to me in my past life? (Ask if they were your father, mother, brother, sister, husband, wife, or other.)

- Was there any harm done? Physical, emotional, psychological, spiritual? [Type of Healing Needed Chart (9)]

- What happened? (This is where you will need to use your imagination and psychic senses. Just ask to see, hear, or feel what happened. You can do this for a shorter or longer time. It can be fascinating what you will be able to discover. Just don't get too immersed in the drama, as this is an exercise to help you let go of the issue.)

- What needs to be forgiven? [Limiting Thoughts Chart (14)]

- What belief or thought do I need to let go of? [Limiting Thoughts Chart (14)]

- What belief or thought do I need to replace it with? [Empowering Thoughts Chart (15)]

- Do I need to forgive? [Yes/No and Clearing Signals Chart (1)]

- How do I heal? [Self-Care Chart (19) and Healing Arts Chart (20)]

- What did I learn in that past life? [Empowering Thoughts Chart (15)]

- What do I feel now about the situation? [Feelings Chart (17)]

Be sure to take notes, so you can later reflect on the reading as a whole.

In addition, you can take a few minutes and drop into a meditative state to experience a little of the past life. Relax, breathe, and let yourself float, travel, and then descend. When you gently float to the ground, look at your shoes and then look around.

- What do you see? Hear? Smell? Feel?

- What are you doing while you are there?

- Is anyone else there with you?

- Do you recognize anyone from your current life in your past life?

- What is significant about what is happening?

- Then jump forward to your death. How did you die?

- What was the lesson you were to learn from this life?

When you want to come back, just tell yourself you will float back to your current life. When you land again, look at your shoes. Take a few moments to ground yourself in the present reality.

After your research and meditation, say a prayer to the angels and healing guides asking them to clear you and all concerned. Give thanks for your loved ones and your own healing. As you go about your life, be attuned to any subtle or noticeable changes in your relationships. This can be a powerful exercise.

There are many books available about past lives, but I want to mention my latest favorite, *Old Souls: The Scientific Evidence for Past Lives* by Tom Shroder. He tells the compelling story of Dr. Ian Stevenson, a research scientist and psychiatrist, who studied small children who had past life remembrances and begged to be taken back to their relatives and homes. Dr. Stevenson catalogued his research from three continents over a forty-year period. The author, an avowed skeptic, gradually becomes aware of concrete evidence that supports the theory of reincarnation, while researching and journeying with the doctor. *Old Souls: The Scientific Evidence for Past Lives* is a fascinating read.

HOW TO CLEAR YOUR BODY DIRECTLY USING A PENDULUM

You can also use the pendulum to scan and clear your own body. Just hold it a few inches from yourself starting anywhere you feel tension. When the pendulum notices blocked energy, it will start to spin to clear the energy. Breathe and enjoy the clearing. When it stops, it means the energy is cleared. Then move to the next part of your body that you find needs clearing.

While you're doing the clearing, it's wonderful to say affirmations or a prayer, such as

I am whole, well, cleared, and healed. Thank you,
God/Goddess, for your healing power and love.

Of course, this can be fun to do on a friend. Have your friend lie down, relax, and breathe. You might want to give them a crystal to hold or to put on their heart chakra. Then just take a few moments going from their feet upward to their head. Have the pendulum do the work clearing, while you can be saying in your mind for your friend,

> *You are whole, well, and cleared. Thank you,*
> *God/Goddess, for your healing power and love.*

This can be relaxing and refreshing, and interesting too—to see how the pendulum interacts directly with our bodies.

PATTERNS OF HEALTH

I want to briefly mention two books that approach pendulum healing in unique ways:

- Dr. Aubrey Westlake (who I mentioned in Chapter 2), while practicing medicine using dowsing, searched for a new medical model that would address the physical and spiritual aspects of the whole person. In his book *The Pattern of Health*, he introduces "Therapeutic Patterns" and the fascinating story of how they were developed with Mr. W. O. Wood in 1956. In the appendix of the book, he tells how to re-create the patterns and use them for healing. Dr. Westlake philosophically draws upon the work of Rudolf Steiner, a modern mystic, who saw himself as a spiritual scientist.

- Robert E. Detzler's book *Spiritual Healing* introduces the "Healing Circle," the "Power Symbol," and other "Healing Patterns," which were inspired by stone healing circles and given to him by Spirit. Detzler, drawing upon his metaphysical background, reveals the spiritual basis for these patterns. The patterns themselves contain universal symbols, words, and numbers to help heal us spiritually.

I have only briefly experimented with Detzler's "Healing Patterns," but you might find that they work for you.

CHAPTER 9

Other Intuitive Tools for Healing and Connecting with Spirit

*I go to nature to be soothed and healed, and to have
my senses put in order.*

—JOHN BURROUGHS, naturalist and author

I usually have a pendulum in my pocket or purse. I just like having it with me at all times. It is like a dear friend I can call on in any moment. Often I receive phone calls while out and about, and I answer questions for my sisters and friends. Or, unexpectedly, I find myself irritated or upset at a store clerk; then I can just pull out my pendulum to clear my energy.

But there are other intuitive tools to use for connecting and healing. This chapter will provide a brief introduction to the many ways in which to enhance your intuition and become more fully connected with your High Self and your Higher Power. Receiving synchronistic signs, receiving insights while journaling, connecting with the angelic realm, examining *A Course in Miracles* and other texts, meditating, praying, and opening to the creative life are all gifts from Spirit to help us live a full and beautiful life.

PAY ATTENTION TO SYNCHRONICITIES

Carl Jung coined the word *synchronicities*. I have always loved this word because it explains all those fun, cool coincidences that happen throughout the day. In Robert Moss's book, *Sidewalk Oracles*, he tells many stories and speaks eloquently of Jung and synchronicity. Here's one example of synchronicity. While I was writing on this subject, I'd been dealing with a "tweaked knee," as my chiropractor called it. At the same time I picked up Moss's book, reading from where I stopped before, Robert Moss was writing about his own knee problems.

Synchronicities seem to increase when we pay attention to them. You can almost see the invisible hands that are directing the orchestra. They magically line up. Last week I was looking for a particular photo of my daughter that I used on her birth announcement. I looked through four photo albums but could not find it. When I pushed the photo albums back in the bookshelf, a card fell out, along with a small photo inside. It was the very photo that I was looking for. It was cropped but in good shape, and I added it to her graduation card.

Synchronicities happen all the time. For instance, you might think of a person and wish to see them, but our lives are busy. Surprise! The next day you run into them. What a synchronicity! When this happens, remember to stop your routine and enjoy their company. Perhaps you even have time for a cup of tea or coffee—better yet, a meal to linger over.

You might need something, and suddenly there it is on the sidewalk. For instance, a beautiful brown couch, ready to take home, appears the day after your roommate moved out, taking her own couch with her!

Or you want to go on a trip to Mexico, and a good friend offers you an all-expense paid trip. Or your grandfather, who is losing his mental faculties, accidentally calls you the day before he dies.

Just for fun, ask Spirit what She would like you to do with your day. Ask the angels to arrange a synchronistic play day. Open your mind and let yourself hear their voices. See where you are led. Whom could you call to give a spiritual lift? Should you turn right or left or go straight? Do you want to go to the ocean, the river, or the mountains? Where will the angels lead you? To what synchronicities?

Appreciate where you live, whether it is a valley, along the coast, or in the mountains. Be grateful for the flowers, plants, and trees. Is there a river, lake, or an ocean nearby? Take a moment to smell the fresh air.

Listen for the sounds of birds. Mindfully attend and go where you are led. This can be a lot of fun if you find yourself alone. Notice the gifts, the synchronicities Spirit brings to you.

Synchronicities are like mini-miracles that can add such a profound feeling of connection to Spirit and to friends. As Robert Moss describes it, "The universe just got personal." Remember to be mindful and give thanks to the creators for your synchronicities.

JOURNAL

Early morning is the magic hour, when it's quiet, while others are still asleep. This is time you can spend with yourself, waking gently. With coffee or tea or water in hand, I go to my purple meditation chair that overlooks the San Lorenzo River. Usually my cat, Pangaea, sits right in front of me.

I watch the river, which has been flowing fully and freely all spring. Over the months I have seen the leaves turn green, and I have also seen my sweet pink eucalyptus felled in a rainstorm. I notice the birds—mallards, blue jays, chickadees, and sometimes a grey heron flying low on the water.

I open a journal and pick up a pen. I let stream of consciousness flow onto the page. I let myself write about all the details of my life, whether happy or sad, joyful, or fearful. I write about my friends, my children, about love and hate, about irritations and frustrations. I write about the previous day, about who said what, and who did what, and why it bugs me so much. Sometimes poems come through. After I clear away all my distractions, new ideas for projects or classes open into my unobstructed consciousness.

After doing this awhile—I've been journaling since my early twenties—I feel I have a knowing about myself. I feel more real to myself. It helps me understand what upsets me, what I like, who I like, and what I want for myself in the future.

Then I use the pendulum and charts to ask any questions I might have about my life. I ask about my health, what I need, and what exercise would be best. I also sometimes clear my adult children, any loved ones who've asked for clearing, and clients who are going through a difficult time.

When I ran my own company, I took care of projects and employees and then went home to my children and husband to take care of us all. I would feel I had lost myself. But if I wrote even a page in the morning, the pen and paper would help me recover myself again.

The writing process comforts me. I write with pen and paper the old-fashioned way. There is something about the simple process that can be taken anywhere, no computer needed, that helps the mind settle down. Plus, I'm not getting distracted by Facebook and Google.

Writing has supported me to have a place to ask Spirit for help, help, help. For friends, family, and myself. My journal is a place to write down wishes and prayers and dreams for others and myself. Sometimes I take these written requests and put them in my prayer box. Later I open it up and read the prayers. Over time every prayer is answered.

My life has not always been so idyllic, but I have managed to journal, pray, and make a place for quiet time in the morning. It's a big secret in life—those who take fifteen minutes of quiet time in the morning will have more of a Spirit-directed synchronistic day and life. See Julia Cameron's book *The Artist's Way* for more details on using the journaling process for healing.

As the author and artist Sark says about journaling in her book, *Living Juicy: Daily Morsels for Your Creative Soul*, "Fill it with inspiration and rage and tears and boredom and chaos and random pieces that happen to float past while you dream on the moonlit night."[30]

CONNECT WITH THE ANGELIC REALM

I teach a class titled "Sacred Meetings with Your Angels" during the end-of-year holidays to give people a chance during the Holy Days to meet

---

[30] Sark, *Living Juicy: Daily Morsels for Your Creative Soul* (Berkeley, CA: Touchstone, 1997), 26.

and learn more about their angels. I also teach a four-week class based on the book *Ask Your Angels* by Alma Daniel, Timothy Wyllie, and Andrew Ramer. I truly love it because in my class my clients do have a personal experience of their guardian angels. They learn the name of their angel, discover how they could communicate more effectively with their angels, and receive a personal message. During the month we all seem to get closer to our angels.

Teaching the class allows me to receive a healing and confirmation because the stories are always so individual. One woman, who is feisty and colorful, has an angel named Zip. She is going through a healing challenge, and Zip is always lightening her up. Another woman's angel's name was surprising—Joe. A widow, she said that she never feels lonely because she feels Joe and her late husband with her.

We have fun with the exercises from the *Ask Your Angels* book—which I highly recommend. You can do the exercises at your own pace or form a small group and do them together. There is true power in spiritual groups.

Here is a shortened process that, if followed, will enable you to meet and greet your angels:

First, you need to clear any blocks that you might have regarding a belief in angels. You can make a list of any beliefs that might be standing in the way of your having an experience with them. Many people have thoughts such as "Angels are not real, or only children believe in angels." "I'm scared. What if they are real?" or "Who am I to be helped by angels?" Once you have the thoughts down, crumple your paper, throw it away or burn it (safely), and then clear yourself with the pendulum. Next, write all the reasons you'd like to connect with your angels. Keep that list and put it in a special place for prayers such as a prayer box.

The second step is to meet your guardian angel. Yes, we all have one. Guardian angels watch over us from before our birth, through our life, and take our soul home to God/Goddess. It doesn't matter whether we see ourselves as an atheist or what our religion is, our guardian angel has been with us our whole life. Wouldn't it be wonderful to meet this most helpful light being?

You can use a centering meditation and after, when you feel at peace, ask to meet and talk to your angel. You can visualize your guardian angel (using your imagination) in your mind's eye. See yourself shaking hands (if you feel more formal) or receiving a hug. Take some time to feel the absolute love of God/Goddess that streams through the angels to you.

You can then ask your angel's name and if they have a message for you. You might pick up your pen and journal and let the message flow naturally. For some, it might take a little while. You can continue meeting with your angels, and one day, you will know their names and be able to hear their messages. It's such a reassuring feeling to be able to communicate directly with the angels.

In the Chapter 5 discussion on Spiritual Guides Chart (4), we met the angels and archangels. You can use the Spiritual Guides Chart to find out who else, besides your guardian angel, you might be talking with. Is it the archangels and their helpers—Raphael, the healer; Uriel, the truth teller; Gabriel, the messenger; or Michael, the protector?

Another way to communicate is with angel cards. Each card in a set of angel cards includes different angels and their messages. My three favorite sets right now are

- Doreen Virtue's *Archangels Oracle Cards*

- Meredith L. Young-Sowers's *Angelic Messenger Cards*

- Kathy Tyler and Joy Drake's *The Original Angel Cards* (from Findhorn)

STUDY A COURSE IN MIRACLES

I've been interested in miracles since I experienced my sobriety transformation. I just knew I wasn't able to stop drinking on my own. I had tried numerous times over a two-year period. Yet, no matter how bad the consequences were, humiliating myself one more time, I couldn't *not* pick up that first drink. When I got sober, I knew a force outside of myself had helped me.

Who hasn't seen a newborn child or animal? It can feel like an opening of the heavens. You experience this awe that a new little perfect creature has come to earth. When you look into their eyes, you can see the wondrous soul of the being.

Earlier in this book, I wrote of "miracles" and how I was introduced to *A Course in Miracles* through a series of synchronistic events.

Even the story of how *A Course in Miracles* began and was written is, in and of itself, miraculous. The book was channeled, dictated by the Voice, to some conservative, scientific people who had worked together for years but were always irritated or angry with each other. The authors, Helen Schucman and William Thetford, Professors of Medical Psychology at Columbia University's College of Physicians and Surgeons in New York City, were tired of the angry and aggressive words that had passed between them for years. William simply said to Helen one day, "There must be another way."[31]

Helen agreed to help them find that way together. Soon after, Helen began receiving messages, dreams, and images that she was to be the "channel" for the book, and William, whom she had never gotten along with, was to be her encouraging and supportive colleague in this joint venture (which took seven years). How their lives changed when they both said *yes*! That is how it began, and the Course was born.

I studied the book when I moved to Unity Village in Missouri and worked in the prayer room. After nine amazing months, I had to leave suddenly to be with my mother, who was dying. After she passed away, I returned to Nevada City, my favorite little town full of old Victorians and large elm and pine trees. Unbeknownst to me, there was a new "Course in Miracles Ministerial Program" just starting. I investigated it,

---

[31] *A Course in Miracles* (Foundation for Inner Peace, Tiburon, CA, 1985), Preface.

applied to be a student, and was accepted. I immediately said *yes* to this synchronistic event and began studying the Course in earnest.

Outwardly, though, it looked as if my life was falling apart. I couldn't find a job, but inwardly I welcomed the time to study, reflect, and internalize the lessons from *A Course in Miracles*. The second book of the three is the *Workbook for Students*, with 365 lessons. Each morning before or after jogging, I continued to read my lesson from the Course and meditated before I started my day.

At that time a second miracle occurred. The loving minister who ran the program believed her students should be dealing with their current life events. Thus, she spent hours with me, counseling me and giving me time to grieve my mother.

A third miracle—she and her husband also ran a bookstore, Books of Harmony. They gave me a part-time job, which provided me a little spending money. (Later, I would help start a shelf of New Age books in a used bookstore in Tahoe City, California. That bookshelf was the beginning of a spiritual group that met for five years. You never know where Spirit will lead you and what Spirit will guide you to do.)

I use the word *miracle* because I was going through such a transition. In one year I left Unity Village, where I had expected to go on living and attend the ministerial program. I wasn't accepted but put on the waiting list. My mother was diagnosed with cancer and six weeks later passed away. Then I found myself once more in Nevada City attempting to find my life. And there it was, another ministerial program studying *A Course in Miracles*, which I loved.

One of the greatest rewards of studying *A Course in Miracles* is that it offers a new way of perceiving yourself and your world. "What Is a Miracle?" says, "A miracle is a correction. It does not create, nor really change at all. It merely looks on devastation, and reminds the mind that what it sees is false. . . . A miracle contains the gift of grace, for it is given and received as one. . . . Forgiveness is the home of miracles."[32]

---

[32] *A Course in Miracles*, Workbook for Students, 463.

I suggest you might benefit from reading Jampolsky's book, *Love Is Letting Go of Fear*, as an introduction and then *A Course in Miracles*. It will have a profound impact on your life. As we are told in the introduction to the book, "This is a course in miracles. It is a required course. Only the time you take it is voluntary."[33]

Why not start now?

USE PRAYER

Prayer is as natural as breathing. Perhaps in this modern world we think it's old-fashioned. In fact, it's probably the most ancient form of solace and healing—human beings in trouble reaching out to the spirit world. When in crisis, most people automatically pray. It is a turning from the material world to the nonmaterial inner world to ask for needs to be met from a higher source.

In A.A. newcomers often don't know to whom they are praying. I was once a newcomer too. I was desperate and knew I couldn't stop drinking and hurting myself. So I said a prayer. A simple prayer—*help me*. It worked. As the Bible says, "Ask and you shall receive."

You don't need to know rationally how your prayer will be answered. You just need to open your mind and heart with faith. You can pray for yourself and others. Pray affirmatively as if the prayer has already been received: "Thank you God/Goddess for my daughter's healing." This will reset your mind to believing that the healing is possible and that your loved one or you are healed.

When you wake up in the morning, pray for others and yourself. Don't forget to pray for yourself. Prayer is not for God/Goddess, who already knows what our needs and wants are. It's to help us align with God/Goddess's power and grace. After praying, it's time to let go and let God/Goddess do his/her work.

Below is a story about heartbreak, prayer, and healing.

---

[33] *A Course in Miracles*, Introduction.

ALWAYS REMEMBER MADYSON MIDDLETON

Do not let the darkness overwhelm the love.

—DEEPAK CHOPRA

In the summer of 2015, a tragedy took place at the Tannery Arts Lofts in Santa Cruz, California, where I live. A vibrant girl, Maddy, only eight years old, was suddenly missing. For two days many of us, and it seemed all of Santa Cruz, searched by the river, into the forest and surrounding environs, and the path to the beach. I prayed for her hourly and asked a number of churches in the area to pray for her too.

After two days the FBI arrived and searched all the lofts, and concurrently a Santa Cruz detective found the body and the perpetrator. Adrian Jerry Gonzalez, known as AJ, a fifteen-year-old boy who was also well known and loved in our community, was apprehended and jailed.

Such a shock. I live in a warm intentional arts community—open, friendly, and diverse. How could this happen to Maddy? It seemed so surreal. How would Maddy's mother, Laura Jordan, survive the death of her beloved daughter? How would AJ's mother, Reggie, survive and live? Many of us knew both the gifted Maddy and the young man AJ, whom we later learned was depressed.

The Santa Cruz community showed their outpouring of love to the mothers, Laura and Reggie, and also the rest of us at the Tannery Arts. Food was donated, and we gathered for nightly potlucks to share our grief. In such a strange, surreal time, it was as if many of us lost our footing. How could this happen in our sweet community?

Laura, Maddy's mother, and Reggie, AJ's mother, saw each other at the makeshift memorial where flowers and candles had been lit. It was two days after learning of Maddy's death. Reggie was sobbing, and Laura, seeing her distress, put her hand on the back of Reggie's head. Truly, that was a miracle. Laura showed amazing powers of love, forgiveness, and calm, and Reggie was brave enough to show up.

Certainly, all of Santa Cruz was grieving. Children, solemnly holding their parents' hands, came to lay their flowers down at a spontaneous memorial site in the heart of the Tannery. Maddy, who had been a popular student at the local elementary school, had many friends.

The memorial service was attended by many residents of Santa Cruz and their children. We were told that just before her death, Maddy had produced and starred in a video about her life at the Tannery. At the service, we all watched Maddy tell her funny and poignant story. Her spirit showed through even on the darkest day.

Later, community-healing clinics were organized at the Tannery with acupuncture, massage, shamanic healing, trauma release, and counseling. The healers donated their time and energy to help us all. We were all very grateful; it helped knowing people cared about all of us when we felt so wounded. Slowly, and at different paces, we healed.

Over the months, Maddy, in spirit, visited my loft three times. I'd be dowsing or meditating and see her in my mind's eye. I'd say "hi" and she'd say "hello." She looked like her bright self, riding in on her Razor (scooter). When I asked her how she was, she'd say, "Oh, I'm fine." She said, too, that she tried comforting her mother, but her mom was distraught. Even so, Maddy was so glad she could visit with her. Then she would say, "bye," and quickly skate away on her Razor.

During these experiences, and in the months that followed, I lit a lot of candles and prayed. I also cleared Maddy using the pendulum and Intuitive Healing Charts. I saw she was taken care of and happy.

"What is the lesson?" I asked the angels. They said, "Love and forgive." I realized I hadn't forgiven the situation when I didn't want to donate to AJ's mother's fund for her relocation and expenses. I wanted to blame someone, something. I wanted to find a rational answer to a tragic, irrational event.

I studied *A Course in Miracles*, prayed for my willingness to forgive, and then made a donation. Reggie left our Tannery community a few months later. Her son is still in the local juvenile hall awaiting his trial and sentencing. Two mothers lost their children that day. Our community continues to heal. Prayer is powerful, healing the saddest, most tragic events.

PRACTICE MEDITATION

Meditation is a simple, natural process to help you relax, focus and, most importantly, get you in tune with your High Self and Spirit. Through quieting your mind and body, you will be able to open a communication channel to receive love and guidance from Spirit.

For many of us, the idea of sitting quietly is painful. Many of us like being busy. In our American culture, we are applauded for checking as many items as we can off our to-do lists. It makes us feel we have accomplished much, that we're going places fast. But many of us are running on empty. We are just whirling, twirling.

When I was visiting my girlfriend on the island of Maui in Hawaii, she and I would notice all the people driving so fast in their usually large cars and trucks. Having just come from the beach where we meditated, wrote in our journals, and took a swim each morning, it seemed comical. She'd say, "Don't they know this is an island? There is nowhere to go except in a circle."

Or we may think we have to take meditation to extremes for it to have an impact. There are some that do silent meditation for twenty-four hours and even meditation retreats for three or seven days or longer. While this may be helpful for those who wish to go deeply into their practice, for the rest of us, we can start slowly. We can learn to meditate at home.

Simply find a quiet place to sit with eyes closed and listen to your own breath moving in and out of your lungs for five minutes a day. Even five minutes can make a difference. Gradually, you can increase this time as you learn to love the process.

GUIDELINES

Here are ideas for helping you create and establish a new meditation habit to incorporate into your day:

- Choose a time and make it as regular as possible, so it becomes a positive habit—morning to start your day off right, noon for added energy and creativity, or bedtime for a calming connection to Spirit before you sleep.

- Any time is a good time to meditate. If you wake up in the middle of the night, you can practice these techniques to calm yourself. In the beginning, it is important to establish a time that you meditate every day so that you establish and maintain the habit.

- Create a warm, loving, comfortable place that is quiet and relaxing. It can be a rocking chair, an easy chair, or a couch. It is nice if you have a few favorite pictures, flowers, or candles around. This is your sacred space where you remember who you truly are—a creative son or daughter of God/Goddess.

- In the Western tradition, you can sit in a comfortable chair to meditate. Just make sure it supports you so that you can sit up straight and relax.

- Many Eastern traditions emphasize a straight spine to keep you alert and present, and to keep the energy in your body flowing during your meditation time.

- If you are sitting in a chair, attempt to keep your feet on the ground. You can take your shoes off if you want. This is to ground your energies into the earth and help you stay centered.

- When you're beginning, it is helpful to read an inspirational thought, prayer, or a line from a book. This helps you slow down, focus on the positive, and prepare for quiet time.

- In the beginning, practice for five minutes and gradually build up to fifteen minutes daily. Increase the time as you become more comfortable and inwardly still. You will begin to look forward to the break in your day.

- Meditation works even though the mind is chattering on and on. Bring yourself back to the breath again and again, or the words. Even if you are having a difficult time doing this, meditation will improve your life. Meditation is simple. Consistently showing up to meditate is the hard part.

- There are many rewards—a clear focused mind and a healthier body. In the process of quieting the mind, we connect and align with Spirit. We open the door and Spirit rushes in. When we are connected to Spirit, we will be protected and guided, and our days will be more synchronistic, joyful, and fun. In the flow of the day, if you notice you've lost your connection, you can take a break and reconnect.

Breathing Meditation

Begin by focusing on your breath. Breathe in and out through your nose if you can, or mouth if you have a cold. At first, it's good to take a couple of deep breaths and let out the breath with a sigh or sound. Then let your breath find its natural rhythm. As it does, your mind will follow the breath as it flows in and out of your body.

You might notice that your mind wants to wander and wonder. What we may initially experience is a busy mind, full of repetitious thoughts, flying in and out of our awareness. Some of us have terrified minds that just don't want to slow down.

If your mind won't quiet, give it a task to do such as repeating a word that is calming. For example, you can repeat the word *peace*, *love*, or *joy*. Or you can chant a simple phrase, such as "I am a child of

God/Goddess. All is well." Or slowly say a prayer, such as the Serenity Prayer:

God grant me the serenity
to accept the things I cannot change,
the courage to change the things I can,
and the wisdom to know the difference.

Be patient and quietly bring the mind back to the breath and to your words. With practice, you will find your mind calming down.

Body Meditation

In this meditation we focus on how the body is feeling and what is going on with each part. You can do this sitting in a chair, sitting up in a bed, or lying down. Focus on the body and how it feels. Notice any relaxed areas or areas of discomfort. You can breathe into any discomfort.

You can then use your pendulum to clear your body before you begin, especially those parts that seem tense. You can use the Physical Body Chart (7) or move the pendulum over your own body.

When you feel comfortable, start with the toes, wiggling them, and then move the feet. Move your focus slowly up the legs and notice how relaxed or tight your calves are. Move up to your thighs, noticing any tension or release. Go into your pelvic region, slowly up your back, and into your shoulders. Is there any tightness? Breathe into your pelvic region and into the core of your body. Do you need to move your shoulders up and down to relax them? As the breath moves into your abdomen, chest, heart, and lungs, just notice the breath and release any tension. Then move down your arms and into your fingers and up again. Notice your neck and head, and your mouth, ears, eyes, and nose.

Also, you can notice any energy sensations or emotions you might be feeling in your body. Or any colors you might see in your mind's eye. What feels vibrant and what doesn't?

When you finish, spend a few moments breathing and thanking each body part. After all, your body has carried you so far on this journey!

Chakra Meditation

Use the Chakras Chart (6) to discover any blocks in your chakras and to get in touch with the energy and power of the chakras.

First, I focus on each chakra, front then back, and ask the angels of light to clear away any dark or negative imprints, to brighten and bring energy to them. You can do this meditation sitting with or without your pendulum. If I use my pendulum, I just clear with my eyes closed.

Start at the base of the spine and work your way up the chakras:

The first chakra in the pelvic region is the bright, earth red energy. Give yourself an energy bath of life force. The color expands in your pelvis, flowing down your legs, and then filling your pelvic region, the core of the body, back, shoulders, and down the arms. Then the earth red energy moves up again into your shoulders, filling your head and spilling over into your aura.

Next, see the second, or sacral, chakra, related to sexuality and creativity, located in your lower abdomen, clearing and filling with bright orange light.

The third, or power, chakra in your solar plexus is related to self-esteem and fills with a bright yellow.

The fourth, the heart chakra, is related to love. See it flow with pale green and sometimes pink colors.

The fifth, the throat chakra, related to communication with others and the self, opens and expands with a beautiful blue.

The sixth, the third eye, related to intuition, is indigo, a lovely dark blue.

The seventh chakra, the crown, is located on top of the head and is a beautiful violet color. This is where you connect with your High Self and Higher Power.

End with light and love showering from above.

You will feel much brighter after your color and chakra bath in which the angels have cleared you. What a perfect way to start the day. Don't forget to thank your angels!

GET OUT OF YOURSELF

Help those less fortunate than you. Just taking a few moments to talk to an older person can make you feel better. I was in our local drug store, and the employees wouldn't help a woman attempting to use the blood pressure machine. Seeing her struggling, I interceded and asked them to help her, but still they wouldn't. So I decided to help her myself! As she sat down, I read the directions and together we did the test. Her blood pressure was high, and she did need to go to the doctor. Repeatedly she said, "Thank you, thank you so much."

If you're feeling sorry for yourself, give money or food to a homeless person on the street. It can be such a relief to get out of yourself.

SPEND TIME IN NATURE

Yes, outside our door lies the healing power of nature. Who has spent time in their garden and not felt better? Even if you're just pulling weeds, raking, or watering, don't you feel better just giving yourself the gift of fresh air and breathing in the energy of plants and trees?

Sometimes when you're sad, hugging a tree can feel good. There they are standing all our lives—oxygenating the air, providing shade, food, and more. They bless us daily, so give them a squeeze and thank them. They appreciate the hugs too.

Venturing further from home, who has not had their soul revived by nature's oceans, rivers, lakes, streams, and the landscapes of foothills and mountains? If you are feeling discouraged, it's time to visit your own power spot on the planet. Mine is Lake Tahoe—the healing waters, pine forests, and majestic mountains encircling the lake.

I've long wanted to travel to Norway, but here I am writing. Yesterday, I took a break and spent just thirty minutes enjoying a film of a cruise of Norway's coast from Bergen to the Arctic Circle. So, if you're house-bound, remember you can be an armchair traveler. It will lift your spirit.

To help you feel closer to and to develop your relationship with nature, read Catriona MacGregor's book, *Partnering with Nature*. She has a way of making you feel comfortable venturing out, awakening your senses, and attuning to the power of animals, plants, trees, and landscape. As she says in her introduction, "Partnering with nature means opening up to an ongoing conversation, listening and learning from everything— from the smallest living creature to the Earth Herself."[34]

TAKE A VACATION FROM YOUR ILLNESS, YOUR DIS-EASE

For a whole day (or more), just pretend you are 100 percent well. (I know this can be challenging, but give yourself a break.) Take a vacation from your dis-ease and into ease. Don't talk to anyone about doctors, medicines, upcoming or past surgeries, or medical interventions. If it's brought up, ignore the question and change the subject. You have a right to well days. If you're enjoying yourself, feel happy. Let the guilt go.

You can have a stay-at-home vacation. Instead of leaving, walk more around town, have massages, enjoy hot tubs, and take walks. Because you're on vacation,

---

[34] Catriona MacGregor, *Partnering with Nature* (New York, NY: Simon & Schuster, Inc. and Atria and Beyond Words, 2010), x.

eat out a little more and treat yourself a little more. After all, you saved money on gas, not to mention on travel.

Better yet, if you have the money, take a real vacation.

IN BED? CREATE ART LIKE FRIDA

One of my heroes is Frida Kahlo, who suffered first from polio in her childhood and then, when she was a teenager, from a debilitating streetcar accident. She spent much of her life in pain and began her creative life in bed. When she went out, she wore beautiful long skirts, which covered her deformed leg. She attracted the attention of the famous Mexican muralist Diego Rivera, showing him her early portfolio. Together they created a vibrant, authentic artistic style for all of Mexico and eventually became famous worldwide. Their love affair, fights, and breakups were legendary—the couple married, divorced, and then married again.

When you see Frida's art, you experience her pain. Although overshadowed by her husband in life, posthumously Frida has become the more famous of the two. Her work hangs in the Louvre in Paris and the Metropolitan Museum of Art in New York. She was not afraid to tell the truth. A year and a few months before her death, she had the first solo show of her work at the *Galería Arte Contemporaneo* in Mexico. Not feeling well, she had her four-poster bed carried to the museum, and she arrived by ambulance!

Two inspiring books for healing through the creative process are Julia Cameron's *The Artist's Way* and John Fox's *Poetic Medicine*. Reading these books will help you find the spirit within to enable you to move from where you are to where you want to go.

Wherever you find yourself in your healing journey, whatever age or circumstance, know that you can pick up a pen or a paintbrush and create like Frida.

CHAPTER 10

Give the Gift of an Intuitive Healing

Every situation, properly perceived, becomes an
opportunity to heal the Son of God.

—HELEN SCHUCMAN,
A Course in Miracles (Introduction)

After continual use, another stage of pendulum dowsing appears of its own accord. When I began giving readings with the pendulum and charts, new psychic aspects of my mind seemed to be opening up. The first time it happened I was amazed. I saw behind my client a large, brilliant white angel. She had a message for my client, "Thank you for all the loving, powerful work you do with the children. We are here to assist you. Please call on us whenever you need us." I did not realize at the time that my client worked professionally as an advocate for children in the court system.

After this experience, it was as if blinders had been taken off my inner eye and I could see into another world. I learned it was clairvoyance, a natural part of my readings. The gift is the ability to see in my mind's eye angels, spirit, symbols, and mini-movies of people's past lives. Later, another psychic gift I became aware of was clairaudience, as I began to hear words and short messages from Spirit while giving readings.

If you practice, you too can become more sensitive and proficient. Your psychic skills—clairvoyance, seeing with your mind's eye, and clairaudience, hearing the still, intuitive voice within—may begin to develop. It can seem natural and inspire awe at the same time, and you will be able to help yourself and others in deeper ways.

PRACTICE ON YOURSELF FIRST

A great person to practice giving Intuitive Healings to is yourself. You are available, willing, and you will be amazed at what you can discover. Or use the buddy system: learn with a friend and practice giving a healing to one another.

To begin, find a comfortable, private place. Give yourself a half hour to an hour so that you have plenty of time. You may want to light a candle to create a sacred atmosphere. Take a moment first to clear yourself and the room.

Say a prayer to call upon Spirit (choose whichever name of God or Spirit you feel comfortable with) to assist in the healing. It can be simple. For instance, "We ask Spirit to guide and direct this healing. Help us to clarify, heal, and resolve these issues. Thank you for your love, help, and guidance."

Before taking action with the insights you have received, check out your intuition with a friend, partner, or mentor. Ask someone who uses the pendulum and Intuitive Healing Charts to verify your answers. The answers are to help you make decisions, but let your rational mind play its part too. This is a gentle, transformative system, allowing you to see all possibilities.

Then when you feel comfortable with using your pendulum and Intuitive Chart, you can give Intuitive Healings to family and/or friends.

GIVE THE GIFT TO ANOTHER

When offering Intuitive Healings to others, remember the purpose of the time spent together is to encourage the best in people. Help them see a broader picture of their life and gently guide them in the direction they want to take. Let it be a positive, life-affirming time that lifts you both to a higher plane.

Listen closely to the person with both your mind and heart. Practice your active listening skills by repeating back to the speaker what you hear. Do not judge; instead, listen carefully as they speak.

I use a clipboard with the Intuitive Healing Worksheet. You can take brief notes on the issues and people that concern them. By writing a few notes, you will be more objective, less emotionally involved; therefore, you will be able to direct the flow of the meeting. But don't get lost in the written details and forget to focus on your client. You may want to make a copy for your friend or client to help them process the healing.

Spend a few minutes helping them clarify their issues and questions so that when you use the pendulum and Intuitive Healing Charts to research, you will receive clear answers.

When you do the research with the pendulum and charts, tell them the answers, so they can reach their own conclusions. To drill down to deeper levels, ask them, "What could this mean for you?" Then you can gently share your insights with them.

Tell them the truth as you see it with love and compassion.

Next, clear them and replace negativity with love and healing for their mind, heart, emotions, and body. This is the most important step.

At the end of the healing, ask, "Do you have any further questions or concerns?"

Be a channel of Spirit's love, compassion, and forgiveness.

Keep tissues handy.

End with a prayer of thanks, knowing that Spirit has worked in your life as well as theirs. *As we give, so we receive.*

After you complete the healing, clear yourself and wash your hands. Give yourself and your client a few minutes to leave this sacred space and re-enter the world. Offer water and drink some yourself.

Hold whatever is said during a healing in confidence.

NOTE

Remember that you are not a doctor or therapist. Sometimes people with complex problems will arrive. Lovingly refer them to others with more experience: perhaps to a doctor, trained therapist, or other professional.

TWO WAYS TO GIVE HEALINGS

The Free Form Healing is a quick method to check for answers. The Intuitive Healing utilizes a worksheet and guides you through a more complete process.

How to Use Free Form Healing

Formulate a question you wish to answer. Write it down for more clarity and begin the following exercise.

Start at either end of the Table of Charts; ask your question while holding the pendulum over the circle in the center.

The pendulum will begin moving toward the name of a chart. Go to this second chart and ask your question again.

Write down your answers.

When you have your answer or answers, return to the Table of Charts, and ask, "What else do I need?" Again you will be led to another chart.

As this process continues, return to the Table of Charts as many times as necessary.

When you return to the Table of Charts and the pendulum stops moving, you will know your question has been answered.

How to Use the Intuitive Healing Worksheet

Clear and center yourself before beginning. Now refer to the Intuitive Healing Worksheet (on page 141). Scan the steps to get an understanding of the process and then walk yourself through until you are familiar with it.

After completing a few healings on yourself and others, you will be more comfortable, and the information will flow. (Make copies of the Intuitive Healing Worksheet for your own use.) This is a simple but profound eight-step process.

Step One What is the primary stress? What are the secondary stresses? Clarify what the real stress is and write about it as a list or a series of questions. [See the Life Stressors Chart (11).]

Step Two What is the underlying cause? (Use the Table of Charts, then guided to other charts.)

Step Three Is there anything blocking the healing? [See the Blocks to Healing Chart (13).]

Step Four Is this due to a present life? Past life? [See the Time and Percent Chart (2).]

Step Five Energetically, where is healing needed in the aura? In the chakras? [See the Chakras Chart (6).] In the body? [See Physical Body (7), Body Systems Chart (8), and Type of Healing Needed Chart (9).]

Step Six Clear and replace: Remember to clear your aura, chakras, body, along with past and present lives. Go back to the Table of Charts and ask: "What is needed to clear or heal this issue?" You will be guided to an answer or answers. [See the Time and Percent Chart (1) and Clearing Needed Chart (16).]

To clear the issue, ask Spirit simply to remove what is blocking you and introduce what will help you. For example, if I learned that behind my anger was fear, I might say a short prayer like this: "In your name and through your power, I ask that fear be removed and replaced with love."

Use your pendulum and watch as it swings in a clockwise direction to clear. When the pendulum stops, you know you are cleared. Take your time to do this most important step.

Step Seven What positive actions can I take to support my healing? Again return to the Table of Charts and ask, "What are my options? What are the solutions? What would be best for me? What would be best for all concerned?" (See the Table of Charts, then be guided to other charts.)

Step Eight Write an affirmation: Use the Empowering Thoughts Chart (15) to create an affirmation or a positive statement that empowers you to accomplish what needs to be done. Write it in the present tense and include your name in the affirmation. End with a short prayer of thanks. [See the Empowering Thoughts Chart (15).]

Again, remember that you are not a doctor or therapist. Recognize when you need to refer someone to others with more experience. After doing a healing for yourself or another, it's a good idea to wash your hands and drink a cool glass of water. Whether you realize it or not, you have been processing and healing deep thoughts and powerful emotions. Pause before you enter life again, take some deep breaths, and give thanks for all your blessings.

Honor the time that you spend healing yourself or others.

The beauty of Intuitive Healings is that you quickly get to the heart of an issue and, by clearing and healing, you release and let a problem go. In this moment, you are free to choose again. In the rhythm of life itself, with its continual cycle of birth, death, and rebirth, your inner self and Spirit can guide you to a new level. Use these methods to give birth to yourself and others again and again.

Remember: *True healing power is within you.*

INTUITIVE HEALING WORKSHEET

Name _____ Date _____

1. What is the primary stress? What are the secondary stresses?

   _____

   _____

2. What is the underlying cause?

   _____

3. Is there anything blocking the healing?

   _____

4. Is this due to a present life? Past life?

   _____

5. Where is healing needed? In the aura? In the chakras? In the body? Anything else?

   _____

   _____

6. Clear and replace. Remember to clear your aura, chakras, body, and past and present lives.

   _____

7. Action. What positive actions can I take to support my healing?

   _____

   _____

8.   *Write an affirmation to support your healing.*

_____

_____

With Spirit all things are possible!

CHAPTER 11

Write Your Own Intuitive Healing Plan

You must find the place inside yourself
where nothing is impossible.

—DEEPAK CHOPRA, *The Seven Spiritual Laws of Success*

What a radical idea that we can create a healing plan for ourselves! I always feel empowered when I have a plan to move forward.

Whether we know it or not, we are the experts of our bodies. We live in our bodies, and our bodies are constantly communicating to us what is needed through feelings, sensations, joy, and pain. For instance, our bodies tell us when we need to rest, wake up, eat food, or exercise; they also tell us what they need for healing. We need to listen and take appropriate action.

In many ways we've been taught to ignore the body. With alarm clocks, demanding schedules, long commutes, overwork, and sometimes the wrong work, we lose touch with ourselves. We forget what is important. But if we listen, we can hear what our amazing bodies are telling us.

Using the pendulum, we can ask and find solutions using the Intuitive Healing Charts.

But why create a plan? Why write it down?

I believe in the power of the word to manifest that which you desire. When you write down your plan, you give yourself permission, you empower that which is inside you, and you help guide yourself on your healing journey. If you use the power of the word and write, you are invoking the universe to help you fulfill the plan. It's simple:

Copy the Intuitive Healing Plan on the following pages.

Ask for your Higher Power and angels to help you as you're creating the plan. Go for the best and highest for yourself.

After you've completed it, put your plan in a visible place so you can remind yourself of it daily.

THE INTUITIVE HEALING PLAN

Intention (What do you truly desire?)

_____

_____

Challenges (physical, emotional, mental, or spiritual)

_____

_____

Metaphor of the Body

_____

_____

New Belief (For example: I can heal! I am loved, honored, and God/Goddess's will for me is perfect health.)

_____

_____

Daily Self-Care (For example: exercise, yoga, meditation, or quiet time)

_____

_____

_____

Weekly Self-Care (For example: massage, beauty treatment, or classes)

_____

_____

_____

Healing Arts Support and Treatments (For example: massage therapist, chiro-practor, or medical doctor)

_____

_____

_____

Friends and Family Support (It's so important to remember people love and care about you!)

_____

_____

Fun (So essential everyday. Something to lighten you up!)

_____

_____

Wishes (Yes, ask your fairy godmother and angels, and see what comes!)

_____

_____

What Is the Gift in This Hardship?

_____

_____

Commitment

_____

_____

Affirmation (Write a truthful, powerful statement to light your way.)

_____

_____

With Spirit all things are possible!

SAMPLE CHART

THE INTUITIVE HEALING PLAN

Intention (What do you truly desire?)
Healing my ears from Tinnitus. Stop the ringing.

Probable Causative Factors
Emotional Stress, PTS, Anxiety

Challenges (physical, emotional, mental, or spiritual)
It's so weird how it never seems to leave. I miss so much my quiet, meditation practice. When stressed, it's so hard to sleep. It's driving me crazy.

Metaphor of the Body
Anxiety made loud. I have suffered from anxiety most of my adult life. It's how I'm wired!

New Belief (For example: I can heal! I am loved, honored, and God/Goddess's will for me is perfect health.)
God/Goddess loves me. I was made perfect by God/Goddess. I will find a way to deal with my stress, anxiety, and find more balance in my life. God/Goddess's will for me is perfect health.

Daily Self-Care (For example: exercise, yoga, meditation, or quiet time)
> Prayer & Meditation
>
> Exercise

Weekly Self-Care (For example: massage, beauty treatment, or classes)
> A.A.
>
> Pedicure
>
> Classes

Healing Arts Support and Treatments (For example: massage therapist, chiropractor, or medical doctor)
> Acupuncture
>
> Chiropractic
>
> Reiki
>
> Find an Integrative MD

Friends and Family Support (It's so important to remember people love and care about you!)
> Adult children, boyfriend, girlfriends, sisters!

Fun (So essential everyday. Something to lighten you up!)
> Swimming, ocean walks, hiking, movies, and travel

Wishes (Yes, ask your fairy godmother and angels, and see what comes!)
> Aligned with my Higher Self and Higher Power
>
> Increased Faith
>
> My living situation is aligned with forces for good.

What Is the Gift in This Hardship?
> Permission to take the best care of me possible!
>
> Finding how much I love acupuncture.

Commitment

I am committed to helping myself heal.

Affirmation (Write a truthful, powerful affirmation to light your way.)

I, a child of God/Goddess, am 100 percent healed. I know in the depth of my being that I am loved.

With Spirit all things are possible!

Remember, no blame, just positive self-love on your healing journey.

CHAPTER 12

Create a Sacred Healing Circle

The greatest healing therapy is friendship and love.
—HUBERT H. HUMPHREY, Politician

It is my hope that after you read this book, you will want to practice becoming more proficient using the pendulum and the Intuitive Healing Charts. What better way to achieve success than to form a small healing group—from two to seven members who meet regularly, either weekly or monthly?

I have been creating and facilitating classes and healing groups for twelve years, and I am always amazed at the spiritual energy, love, and joy that are generated by a group. Magic happens. People are energized, excited, and ready to explore new avenues of healing.

True healing is an ongoing process. In this book I refer to the word *healing* in its broadest sense. What better way than to come together to help each other, clear energy, research the issues, find solutions, and encourage each other, and to help heal spiritually, mentally, and emotionally. People gain confidence to be themselves and transform over time to become their authentic selves.

PRACTICE WITH A FRIEND

If you bought this book and learned how to use the pendulum and charts and you have a friend you'd like to teach, please go ahead. Many friends of mine have learned from friends who have taken a class from me. If you start meeting on a regular basis—once a week is great—then two people can learn much more easily. You can practice with each other and share insights about your healing and life.

My friend Julie and I meet informally once a month. We have helped each other with our healing concerns and in all aspects of our lives. Julie took just one class using the Intuitive Healing Charts and now is a practiced dowser. I have had the pleasure of giving her psychic readings and vice versa.

We use Intuitive Healing Charts when we have health concerns. We center and give each other short readings. We check to see if we are taking the right vitamins, whether we are exercising enough, and whether we need to do more for our health. Additionally, we've asked for each other information about probable results of PAP smears, mammograms, and other medical tests when we are waiting for results.

STRUCTURE FOR THE SACRED HEALING CIRCLE

You can choose for your sacred healing circle to meet once a week, every other week, or once a month. Once you have set a time to meet, it's good to keep the commitment and view it as special, sacred time.

Especially in the beginning, you might want to just invite like-minded friends who will be open to new ideas and already have a belief in the spiritual life.

A day before your scheduled meeting, you might want to send out an e-mail to remind people of the date and time and to bring their pendulum, the Intuitive Healing Charts, and a notebook.

I write out a simple agenda or program outline to keep myself on track, including making any announcements. If you get lost, it gives you a way home.

The space where the group takes place is important. It should be clean, comfortable, and airy—a peaceful place where Spirit and the group can do their work. It's important that the trash is taken out. Angels, spirits, and human beings like being in harmonious, welcoming surroundings that have been imbued with positive energies. So choose the space wisely. It can be your home, office, or another quiet public space.

Clear the room using your pendulum or with incense or sage if you prefer. Sage is a wonderful herb used by Native Americans in all their healing ceremonies. You can find it at your local healing store or online.

Flower Power—It's always wonderful to have healing flowers because they add a touch of nature and elegance.

Prepare tea, water, and healthy snacks. People seem to need a little protein after spiritual work.

Before people arrive, prepare yourself. Ground and ask that the angels of light and love come join you.

It's easier to learn if we have an open, playful attitude and attempt not to take ourselves too seriously. Play relaxes us, engages both sides of the brain, and lifts us to a higher vibration. It also opens the subconscious and helps us integrate all parts of our being. Remember our Creator is infinitely playful.

I created the following guidelines as a starting point. You may want to write your own with your group. Reading the rules at the beginning of the meeting helps reinforce them, and then everyone knows what to expect.

GUIDELINES FOR THE SACRED HEALING CIRCLE

- Our collective intention is to create a place of safety and acceptance for each member to feel the loving and healing power of Spirit.

- We will practice listening and mindfulness while each speaks their truth.

- Cross talk will be minimal. We understand each person is on their healing journey and inwardly knows what is best for themselves.

- Loving feedback, when requested, will be given to enrich the person, never to weaken them.

- Each person sharing will know what they say is held in confidence.

- Love is our code. Spirit is our answer to all our healing needs.

ADVICE FOR THE GROUP LEADER

Just as every person is unique, so every group has its own personality. Usually, there is a core group of dedicated people and some people who come for a short period of time. I like to find out in the first meeting what everyone's needs are and to check in periodically with people to see if their needs are being met. The bottom line is that everyone wants to be heard, respected, valued, and understood. We must learn patience and tolerance with a large dose of compassion.

If you're the group facilitator, it is helpful not to take anything personally. When I wrote this, it made me laugh because that can be difficult. Of course, you want your students happy and the group to be running well, but you can't control all the factors that will influence people and their choices. Give with love and people will accept what they can.

As facilitator or leader, you work with Spirit. Just do as you think your Spirit would have you do. The facilitator is not the "healer"; healing is by God/Goddess. And the facilitator is not the judge/jury. You are there to support in a conscious way the healing activities. Except when requested, and during the process of the Intuitive Healings, you are not looking for solutions for class members. By listening well, you are helping people go within to find their own solutions.

If we are giving up responsibility for our self and depending on someone else, we are making them our god. They are fallible, just like us. Lean on the angels and God/Goddess instead. Bill Wilson, founder of

Alcoholics Anonymous, said, "Make your relationship right with Him, and great things will come to pass."

Often in my groups, even though we discuss deep issues, there is much laughter. To me, it's a sign the angels are with us and that higher forces are in play. Despite outer circumstances that might be unfolding in our lives, joking and laughing are great medicine for the soul. Laughter helps us be humble as children in the loving hands of God/Goddess.

Once in a while a person wants to dominate a meeting. I ask them to leave. (Just kidding.) Usually, I give these people a responsibility, and then they can focus on their own job within the group. Often it means the person does have much to share, but they are, unconsciously or not, doing it in a way that is unbalanced for the group. You can refer back to the class rules. If necessary, speak to this person after class. It can be detrimental to other individuals in the group if one person takes over. Dominating personalities will drive other members away. In the group we are learning to have responsibility for ourselves and our health. What better way to learn than by modeling it in the class?

I see healings happening both quickly and slowly. It can be in an instant or, in most cases, in a day, a week, or a month. Healing is a process, and groups work together with that process. We must let the results go and let God/Goddess do the work.

In summary, the following tips contribute to a successful group experience:

- Use an opening prayer to invite Spirit and angels. (They do the work.)

- Make the group safe and comfortable for all.

- Listen with the mind and heart.

- Allow equal time for each member.

- The process of the group moves forward.

- There is variety and value to keep people motivated to come back.

BEGIN THE SACRED CIRCLE

To begin, I light a candle (green is a great color for healing) and say a simple prayer. You can use the Lord's Prayer (such a powerful incantation), create your own prayer, or use this one:

Angels of Light and Love, and Archangels,
Mary and Jesus,[35]
Thank you for your ever-healing presence.
Be with us today and always.
Open our minds and hearts to new ideas and resources.
Clear our erroneous thoughts and beliefs.
Help us let grievances go and let only Love be present.
Let us remember we are always loved, never alone.
We affirm that God/Goddess's will for us is complete healing on all levels.
Thank you, Spirit, for your sustaining, ever-present Love.

GROUNDING MEDITATION

The facilitator or another member of the group can lead the grounding meditation found in Chapter 9. Often many of us are ungrounded, especially because of our busy lives—unconnected with the earth, our bodies, and our spiritual support. That is when accidents can happen. It is hard to manifest healing when a part of us is not in our bodies. We need to be present to win.

At Unity Village, our minister used to raise her voice and say, "Never leave home without praying! It can save your life."

READ THE GUIDELINES FOR THE SACRED CIRCLE

Reading the guidelines for the sacred circle is a simple way to reinforce the intention of the group and make sure everyone understands the ground rules.

---

[35] You can name and call in your own favorite guides.

CHECKING IN

In groups I lead, I like to give people the opportunity to tell what is happening in their lives. This gives them a chance to become present if anything exciting is happening or if there is something weighing on their minds. Usually, checking in takes three to five minutes per person, and sometimes you have to remind the group that this is a short check-in. This is a great time for all to practice mindful listening, focusing on the speaker, but refraining from giving feedback. This allows the speaker the freedom to say what is on their mind without being given solutions.

FOR NEW GROUPS

Initial meetings can be used to review and familiarize everyone with using the pendulum and the individual charts. I like to go through three to five charts per meeting. Everyone can practice, ask questions, and learn the multiple ways the charts can be used.

In a later meeting, review Chapter 10. You can read, review the process and worksheet, and answer questions. The group leader can demonstrate how to do healings using the Intuitive Healing Charts and worksheet. As the facilitator is walking students through the process, some members also check the answers they receive via Free Form Healing with the pendulum. Remember there are two primary ways to give healings: the Free Form Healing, which is a quick method to check for answers by going right to the charts you know are needed; or the more complete Intuitive Healing, which utilizes a worksheet and guides you step by step. (Remember to make copies for the group.)

In closing the group, you can stand and create a small circle. I always say a short closing prayer, and others in the group join in with their thoughts or prayers too. If the group is large, I ask for one word representing their experience in the group. In the end, it's almost like a poem and we close the sacred circle.

IN CLOSING

I wish you much success on your healing journey. Remember, each of us is unique and has a different healing path. Today, there are many resources available to help us heal. Find what works best for you.

While you're in the mystery, remember to give yourself radical self-love, as you would love a child who needs your support. No blame! Keep seeking that which brings you health, life, creativity, and joy. *Remember, you are worthy and deserving of miracles and healing.*

I will be holding the space for self-knowledge, healing, and love for us all.

ACKNOWLEDGMENTS

I felt honored by the angels and spirit guides who urged me to write this book. Thank you for your inspiration, ideas, and clarity.

To the talented and creative Judika Illes, my editor, who was kind and patient during the writing process. To the Red Wheel/Weiser Publishing editors, graphic artists, and staff for bringing this book to life and into the world. It was a soul-satisfying experience to work with them and to add to their extensive library of books. To my agent, Rita Rosenkranz, who helped me find just the right publisher and worked so diligently on the contract.

I learned much from those who have come before me and alongside me on this journey through their books: Charles and Myrtle Fillmore, Robert Dexler, Louise Hay, Deepak Chopra, Caroline Myss, Lissa Rankin, C. Norman Shealy, Julia Cameron, and many, many more healers and writers, all visionaries in the mind, body, and spirit realm.

To my Spiritual Response Therapy teacher, Shakti Wilson, who helped heal me and taught me so much.

To my many clients who risked, opened their hearts, and shared their lives and stories with me.

To Michael Larsen, founder of the San Francisco Writers Conference and to the attendees at Women Writing in the Redwoods Retreat, who gave me practical advice and much encouragement to start, write, and finish this book. To my author coach, Nina Amir, who, by example and word, urged me to blog, write, and publish. To Jordan Rosenfeld, who said, "Just write your book!"

To Magdalena Montagne, my editor; Thea Crossley and Juanita Usher, my readers; and Magdalena's circle of poets who honor the word, speak words of grace and honesty, and continue to teach me so much.

To Catherine Segurson, founder of the *Catamaran Literary Reader* and the Catamaran Writing Conference, who is such an example of grace, art, and persistence.

To my first students in my Pendulum Healing Course class, Margaret Niven, Marion Blair, Elizabeth Sosa Castenda, Deanie Hochman, Tony Khurana, and Lynora Iwine, who taught me so much and gave me suggestions for the charts.

To the Tannery Arts and ArtSpace who provided me with a creative home.

To my children, Danielle and Adam Torvik-Staffen, and sisters, Laurie Carah and Therese Moldvay, who encourage me, share the journey, and give their love.

To my friend Walt Froloff, who daily said, "Write" and "Have you blogged today?"

Thank you!

RECOMMENDED READING
AND BIBLIOGRAPHY

Angels

Daniel, Alma, Wyllie, Timothy, and Ramer, Andrew. *Ask Your Angels*. New York: Random House, 1992.

Moolenburgh, H. C. *A Handbook of Angels*. Essex, England: C. W. Daniel Company Limited, 1988.

Chakras and Auras

Ambrose, Kala. *The Awakened Aura*. Woodbury, MN: Llewellyn Publications, 2011.

Myss, Caroline. *Anatomy of the Spirit*. New York: Crown Publishers, 1996.

Myss, Caroline. *Why People Don't Heal and How They Can*. New York, NY: Harmony Books, 1997.

Communication

Rosenberg, Marshall. *Nonviolent Communication: A Language of Life*. Encinitas, CA: Puddle Dancer Press, 2005.

Dreaming and Synchronicity

Moss, Robert. *Dreamways of the Iroquois: Honoring the Secret Wishes of the Soul*. Rochester, VT: Destiny Books, 2005.

Moss, Robert. *Sidewalk Oracles*. Novato, CA: New World Library, 2015.

Energy Medicine

Bartlett, Richard. *Matrix Energetics: The Science and Art of Transformation*. New York, NY: Simon & Schuster, Inc., 2007.

Cointreau, Maya. *The Comprehensive Vibrational Healing Guide*. Roxbury, CT: Earth Lodge, 2013.

Eden, Donna. *Energy Medicine*. New York, NY: Penguin/Putnam, 1998.

Gerber, Richard. *Vibrational Medicine*. Rochester, VT: Bear & Company, 2001.

Kaminski, Patricia, and Katz, Richard. *Flower Essence Repertory*. Nevada City, CA: Flower Essence Society, 1999.

McIntyre, Anne. *Flower Power*. New York, NY: Henry Holt & Company, Inc., 1996.

Shealy, Norman. *Energy Medicine*. Virginia Beach, VA: 4th Dimension Press, 2011.

Feelings

Froloff, Walt. *Learning Elephant: Using the Power of Applied Feelings Intelligence*. Aptos, CA: Patent Alchemy Press, 2009.

Health and Healing

Brennan, Barbara Ann. *Hands of Light: A Guide to Healing Through the Energy Field*. New York, NY: Bantam Books, 1988.

Chopra, Deepak. *Reinventing the Body, Resurrecting the Soul*. New York, NY: Random House, 2009.

Fox, John. *Poetic Medicine*. New York, NY: Penguin, Putnam, 1997.

Hay, Louise L. *You Can Heal Your Life*. Carlsbad, CA: Hay House, Inc., 1984.

Hover-Kramer, Dorothea. *Healing Touch*. Boulder, CO: Sounds True, 2011.

Loyd, Alexander, with Johnson, Ben. *The Healing Code*. New York, NY: Hachette Book Group, 2010.

Myss, Caroline. *Why People Don't Heal and How They Can*. New York, NY: Harmony Books, 1997.

Ni, Maoshing. *Secrets of Longevity: Hundreds of Ways to Live to Be 100*. San Francisco, CA: Chronicle Books, 2006.

Rankin, Lissa. *Mind Over Medicine*. Carlsbad, CA: Hay House, Inc., 2013.

Targ, Russell, and Katra, Jane. *Miracles of Mind*. Novato, CA: New World Library, 1999.

Intuition

Peirce, Penney. *The Intuitive Way*. New York, NY: Simon & Schuster, Inc., Atria and Beyond Words, 2010.

Life After Death

Jackson, Laura Lynne. *The Light Between Us*. New York, NY: Spiegel & Grau, 2014.

Shroder, Tom. *Walking in the Garden of Souls*. New York, NY: Penguin Putnam Inc., 2001.

Magic

Illes, Judika. *The Big Book of Practical Spells*. Newburyport, MA: Red Wheel/Weiser, 2016.

Medical Intuition

Nani, Christel. *Diary of a Medical Intuitive*. Palm Springs, CA: Queens Court Press, 2004.

Shealy, Norman. *Medical Intuition: Awakening to Wholeness*. Virginia Beach, VA: 4th Dimension Press, 2010.

Zion, Tina. *Become a Medical Intuitive: The Complete Developmental Course*. Omaha, NE: Writelife Publishing, 2012.

Meditation

Kornfield, Jack. *Meditation for Beginners*. Boulder, CO: Sounds True, 2004.

Nature

MacGregor, Catriona. *Partnering with Nature*. New York, NY: Simon & Schuster, Inc. and Atria and Beyond Words, 2010.

Past Lives

Shroder, Tom. *Old Souls: The Scientific Evidence for Past Lives*. New York, NY: Simon & Schuster, 1999.

Weiss, Brian, and Weiss, Amy. *Miracles Happen: The Transformational Healing Power of Past-Life Memories*. New York, NY: HarperCollins, 2012.

Pendulum Dowsing—Methods and History

Bird, Christopher. *The Divining Hand*. New York, NY: E. P. Dutton, 1979.

Detzler, Robert E. *The Freedom Path*. Snohomish, WA: Snohomish Publishing Company, Inc., 1996.

Detzler, Robert E. *Soul Re-Creation: Developing Your Cosmic Potential*. Redmond, WA: SRC Publishing, revised 1999.

Detzler, Robert E. *Spiritual Healing*. Redmond, WA: SRC Publishing, revised 2008.

Jurriaanse, D. *The Practical Pendulum Book*. York Beach, ME: Samuel Weiser, Inc., 1986. Translated from the Dutch, published in Holland, 1984.

Lonegren, Sig. *The Pendulum Kit*. New York, NY: Simon & Schuster, 1990.

Nielsen, Greg, and Polansky, Joseph. *Pendulum Power*. Rochester, VT: Destiny Books, 1977, 1987.

Webster, Richard. *Pendulum Magic for Beginners*. St. Paul, MN: Llewellyn Publications, 2005.

Westlake, Aubrey T. *The Pattern of Health*. Berkeley, CA and London, England: Shambhala Publications, Inc., 1974.

Willey, Raymond C. *Modern Dowsing*. Phoenix AZ: Esoteric Publications, 1976.

Positive Thinking

Peale, Norman Vincent. *The Power of Positive Thinking*. New York, NY: Simon & Schuster, 2003.

Shamanism

Beery, Itzhak. *The Gift of Shamanism*. Rochester, VT: Destiny Books, 2015.

Harner, Michael. *The Way of the Shaman*. New York, NY: HarperSanFrancisco, 1980.

Ingerman, Sandra. *Soul Retrieval: Mending the Fragmented Self*. New York, NY: HarperSanFrancisco, 1991.

Rysdyk, Evelyn. *Spirit Walking: A Course in Shamanic Power*. San Francisco, CA: Weiser Books, 2013.

Spirituality

A Course in Miracles. Tiburon, CA: Foundation for Inner Peace, 1975.

Fillmore, Charles. *Talks on Truth*. Lee Summit, MO: Unity Books, 1912, 2007.

Jampolsky, Gerald G. *Love Is Letting Go of Fear*. New York, NY: Random House, 1979, 2011.

Kornfield, Jack. *A Path with Heart: A Guide Through the Perils and Promises of a Spiritual Life*. New York, NY: Bantam Books, 1993.

Roberts, Jane. *Seth Speaks: The Eternal Validity of the Soul*, reprinted. San Rafael, CA: Amber-Allen Publishing, 1994.

Williamson, Marianne. *A Return to Love: Reflections on the Principles of "A Course in Miracles."* New York, NY: HarperCollins, 1992.

APPENDIX

The Intuitive Healing Charts

Before beginning—center yourself, take a few deep breaths and ask using your pendulum:

- Am I working with my High Self?

- Are my answers 100% correct?

If no, keep clearing until you are ready.

If you are working with another person, always ask first:

- Do I have permission to work with this person?

- Is this for the highest good for this person?

If the answer is no, you can always say a prayer for them and place them in Spirit's hands.

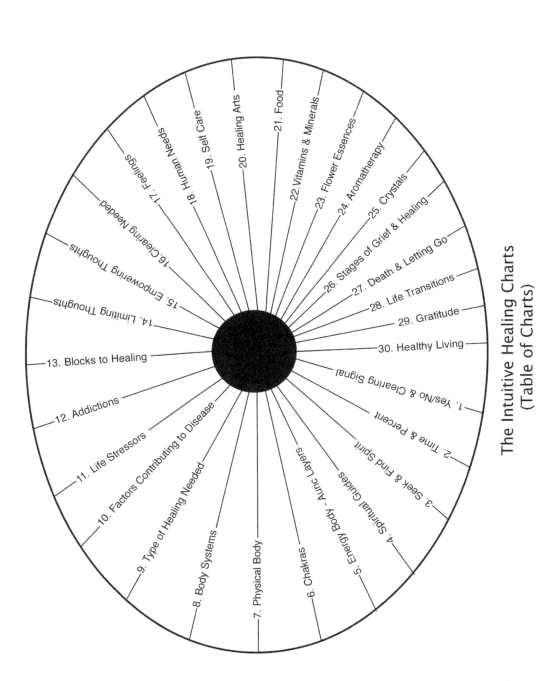

The Intuitive Healing Charts
(Table of Charts)

1. Yes/No & Clearing Signal
2. Time & Percent
3. Seek & Find Spirit
4. Spiritual Guides
5. Energy Body - Auric Layers
6. Chakras
7. Physical Body
8. Body Systems
9. Type of Healing Needed
10. Factors Contributing to Disease
11. Life Stressors
12. Addictions
13. Blocks to Healing
14. Limiting Thoughts
15. Empowering Thoughts
16. Clearing Needed
17. Feelings
18. Human Needs
19. Self Care
20. Healing Arts
21. Food
22. Vitamins & Minerals
23. Flower Essences
24. Aromatherapy
25. Crystals
26. Stages of Grief & Healing
27. Death & Letting Go
28. Life Transitions
29. Gratitude
30. Healthy Living

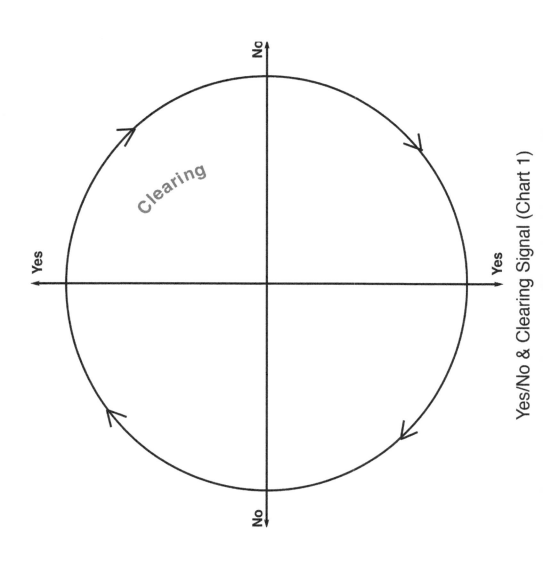

Yes/No & Clearing Signal (Chart 1)

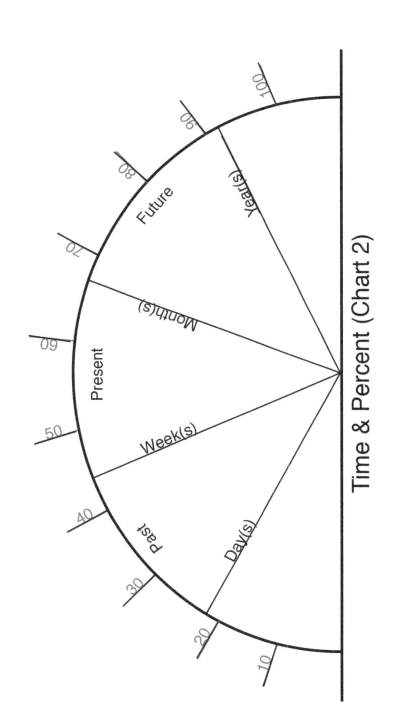

Time & Percent (Chart 2)

Seek & Find Spirit (Chart 3)

- Practice Mindfulness
- Daily Spiritual Practice
- Seek Spiritual Answers
- Let Go of the Past
- Ask Forgiveness
- Clean Up the Past
- Spiritually Surrender
- Ask for Support
- Realize the Truth
- Become Aware

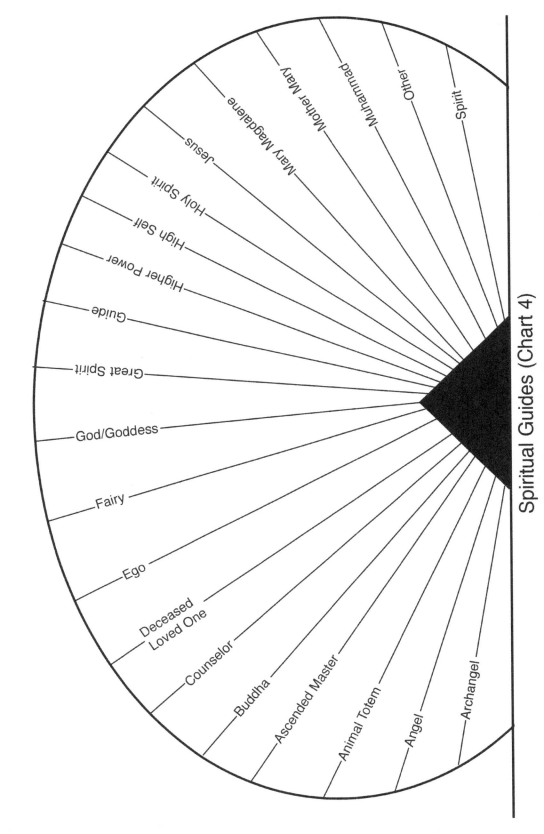

Spiritual Guides (Chart 4)

Spirit
Other
Muhammad
Mother Mary
Mary Magdalene
Jesus
Holy Spirit
High Self
Higher Power
Guide
Great Spirit
God/Goddess
Fairy
Ego
Deceased Loved One
Counselor
Buddha
Ascended Master
Animal Totem
Angel
Archangel

Energy Body - Auric Layers (Chart 5)

Ketheric Body

Celestial Body

Etheric Body Template

Astral Body

Mental Body

Emotional Body

Etheric Body

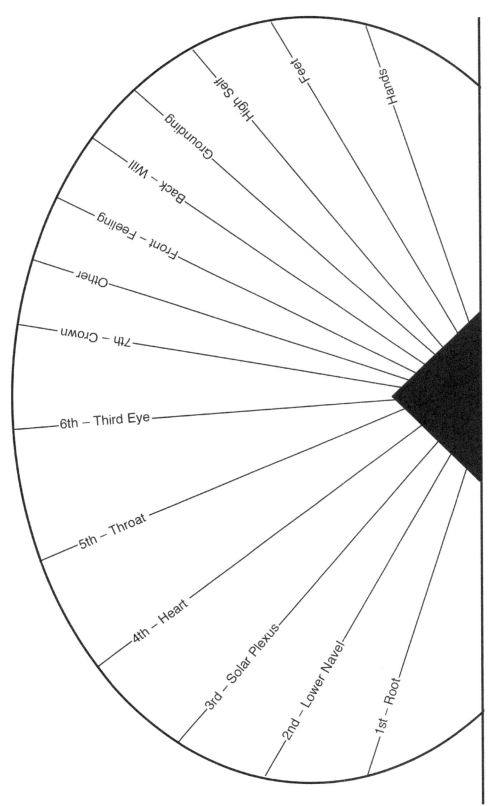

Chakras (Chart 6)

Physical Body (Chart 7)

Body Systems (Chart 8)

- Skeletal Articular
- Respiratory
- Reproductive - Male
- Reproductive - Female
- Renal
- Nervous
- Muscular
- Lymphatic
- Integumentary (skin)
- Immune/Lymphoid
- Endocrine
- Digestive
- Cardiovascular

Type of Healing Needed (Chart 9)

Spiritual

Physical

Mental

Emotional

Combination

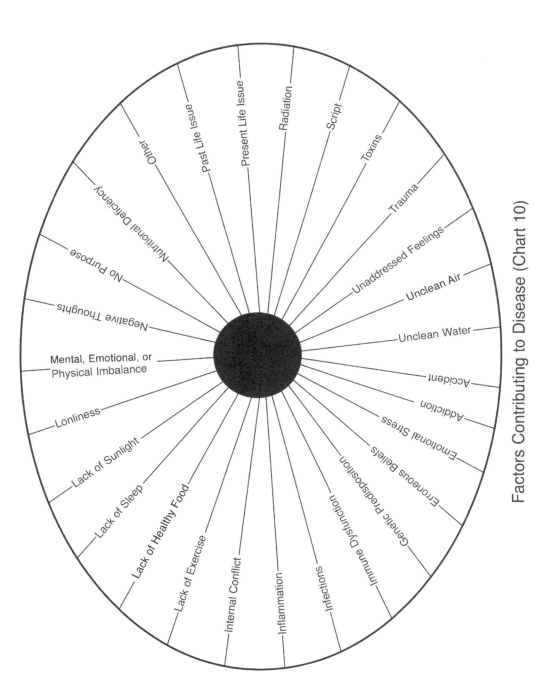

Factors Contributing to Disease (Chart 10)

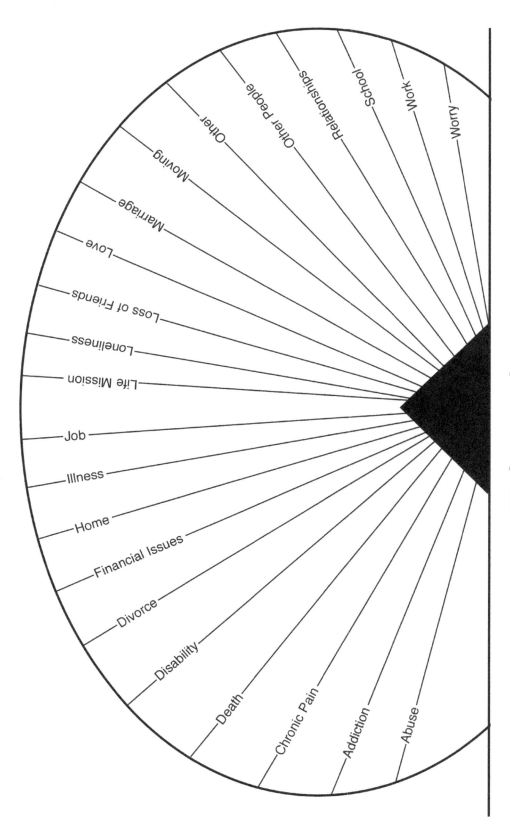

Life Stressors (Chart 11)

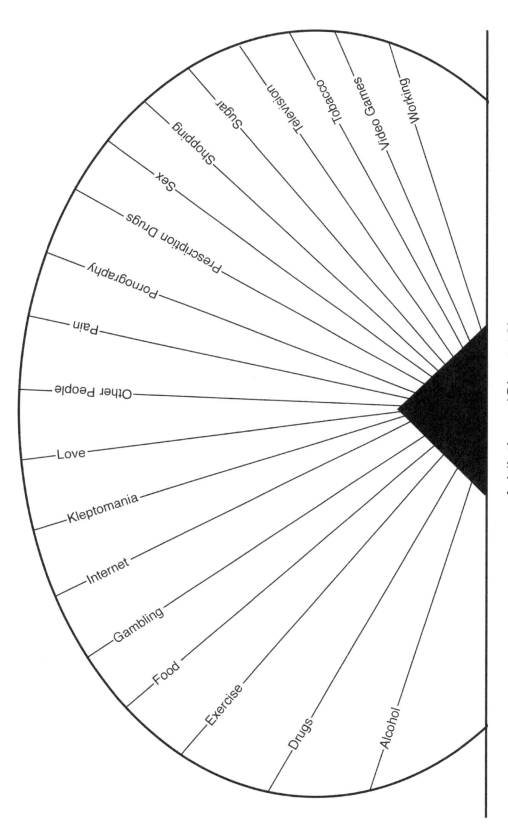

Addictions (Chart 12)

Blocks to Healing (Chart 13)

- Woundology
- Unworthiness
- Unforgiveness
- Separation from Spirit
- Present Life Trauma
- Past Life Trauma
- Other
- Negative Pleasure
- Identity
- Holding on to the Past
- Fear
- False Belief
- Control Issues
- Bitterness

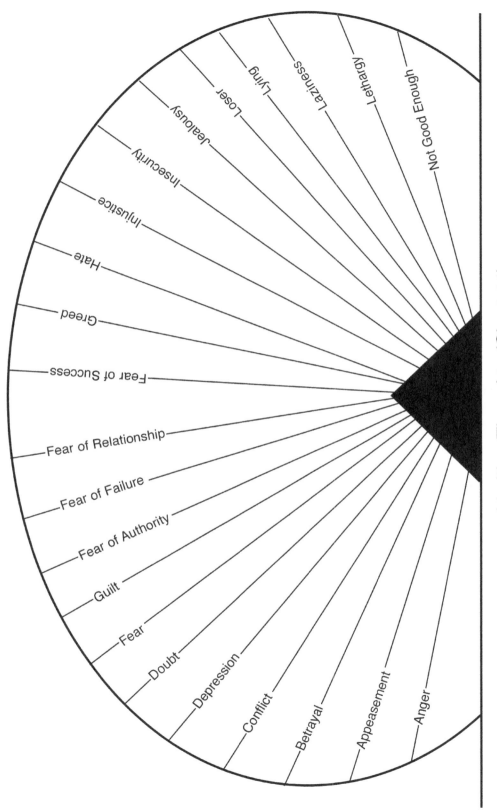

Limiting Thoughts (Chart 14)

Empowering Thoughts (Chart 15)

Clearing Needed (Chart 16)

Self – Spirit
Self – Mind
Self – Emotions
Self – Body
Room
Object
Land
House
Group
Gallery/Store
Friend
Family Member
Class
Car
Business

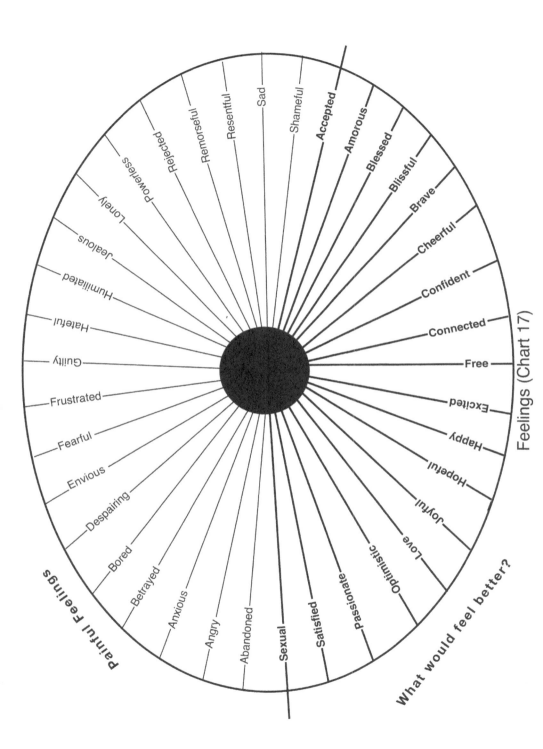

Feelings (Chart 17)

Painful Feelings

What would feel better?

Accepted
Amorous
Blessed
Blissful
Brave
Cheerful
Confident
Connected
Free
Excited
Happy
Hopeful
Joyful
Love
Optimistic
Passionate
Satisfied
Sexual

Abandoned
Angry
Anxious
Betrayed
Bored
Despairing
Envious
Fearful
Frustrated
Guilty
Hateful
Humiliated
Jealous
Lonely
Powerless
Rejected
Remorseful
Resentful
Sad
Shameful

Human Needs (Chart 18)

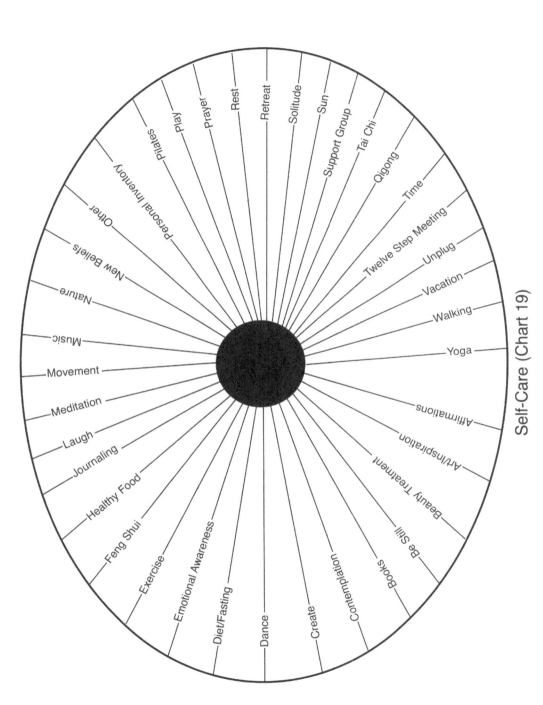

Self-Care (Chart 19)

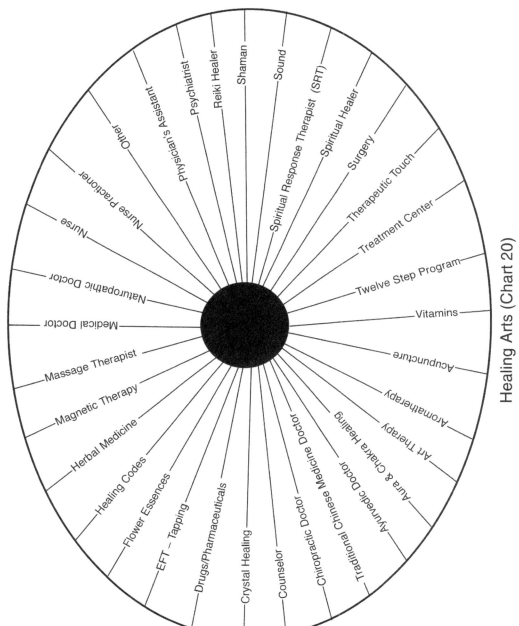

Healing Arts (Chart 20)

Foods (Chart 21)

Vitamins & Minerals (Chart 22)

Healthy Food
Other Mineral
Other Vitamin
Zinc
Vitamin K
Vitamin E
Vitamin D
Vitamin C
Vitamin B
Vitamin A
Multivitamin
Iron
Herbs
Folic Acid
Chromium
Calcium

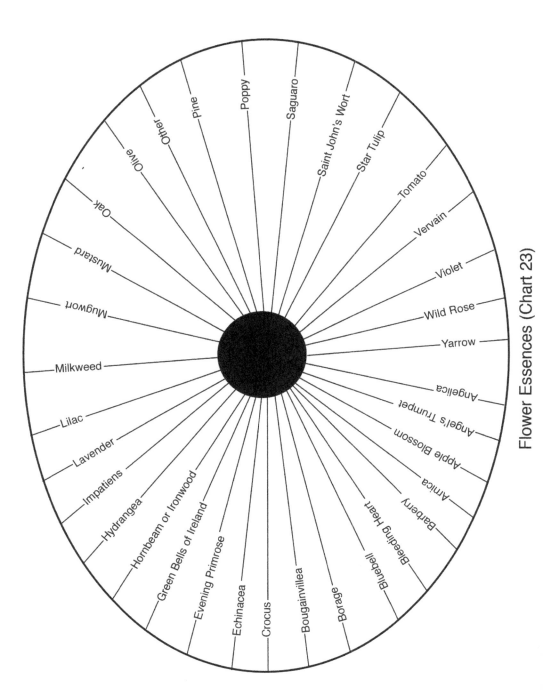

Flower Essences (Chart 23)

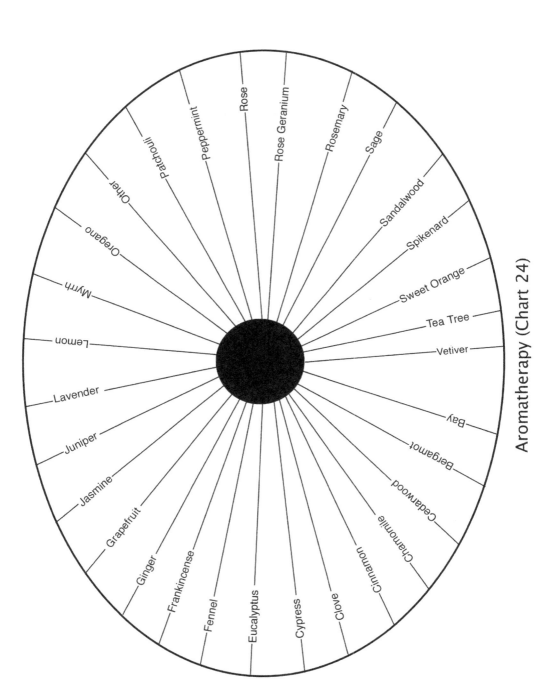

Aromatherapy (Chart 24)

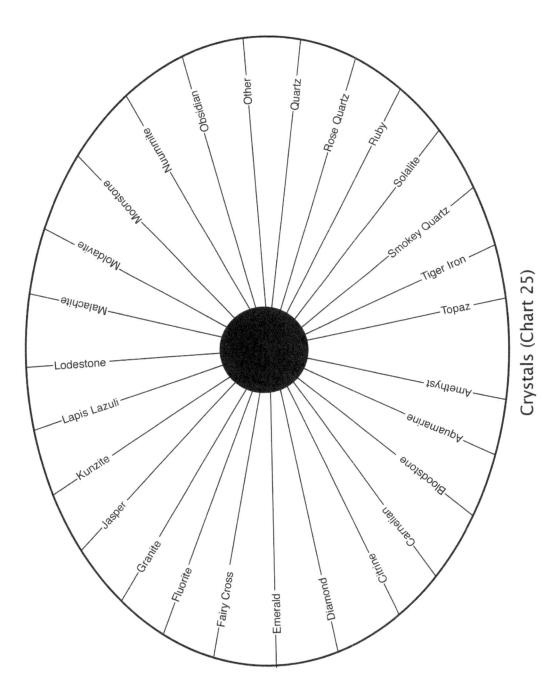

Crystals (Chart 25)

Stages of Grief & Healing (Chart 26)

New Life

Rebirth

Acceptance

Depression

Bargaining

Anger

Denial

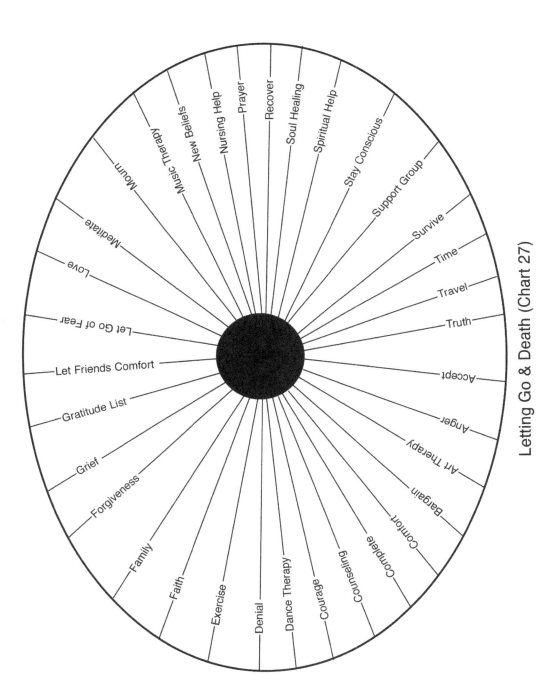

Letting Go & Death (Chart 27)

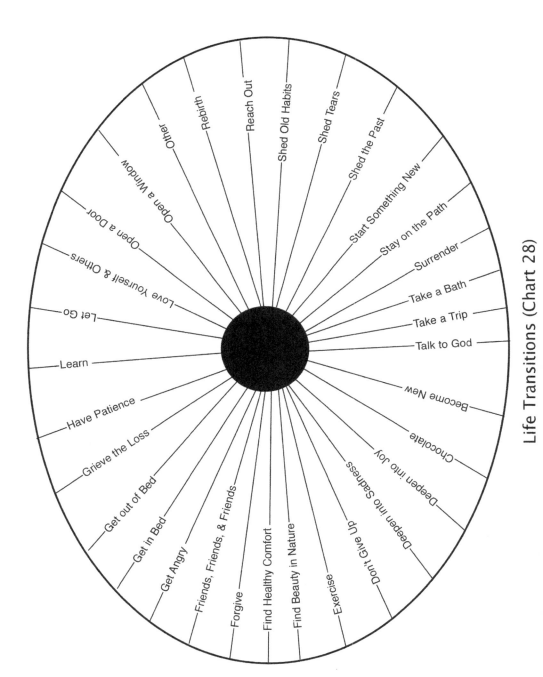

Life Transitions (Chart 28)

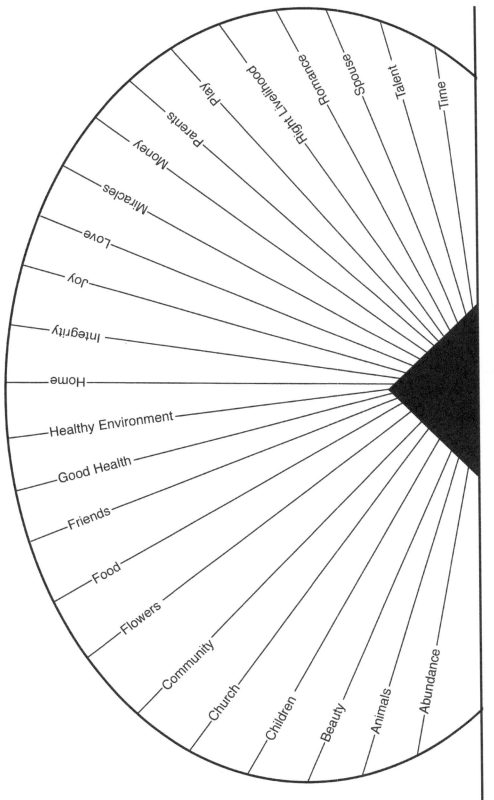

Gratitude (Chart 29)

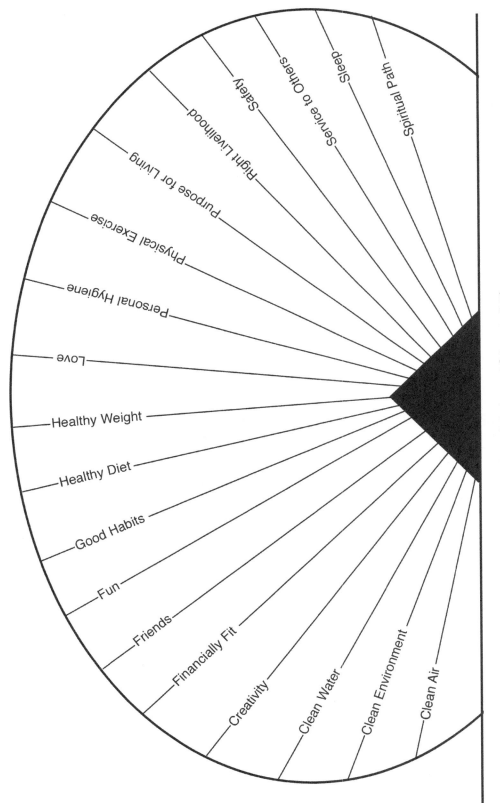

Healthy Living (Chart 30)

ABOUT THE AUTHOR

JOAN ROSE STAFFEN is a writer, artist, and psychic healer. On the spiritual path since her early twenties, she has explored many healing modalities including psychic healing, yoga, meditation, a Course in Miracles, Unity Church principals and prayers, and spiritual response therapy, a dowsing system for deep healing. Currently, she works and plays in an intentional artist community in Santa Cruz, California, called the Tannery Arts Lofts where she provides workshops and psychic healings. Visit her at *www.joanrosestaffen.com.*

TO OUR READERS